TALINGA

The house that Dad built and its role in **saving K'gari**

Margaret Anne Sinclair

Talinga: The house that Dad built and its role in saving K'gari
Author – Margaret Anne Sinclair
© Margaret Anne Sinclair 2025
www.masinali.com

This book is a memoir, written by the author to recount personal experiences, memories and perspectives on various aspects of their life. The content is based on the author's recollection and interpretation of events. By reading this memoir, you acknowledge and accept that personal narratives are inherently subjective, and that the author's experiences and interpretations may not necessarily reflect your own.

By reading this book, you acknowledge and accept the potential triggers associated with discussions about end of life and agree to take responsibility for managing your own emotional well-being while engaging with the content.

All rights reserved. This book may not be reproduced in whole or part, stored, posted on the internet, or transmitted in any form or by any means, electronic or mechanical, or by photocopying, recording, sharing or other means, without written permission from the author of this book. All content found online or offline without written permission is in breach of copyright law and therefore renders you liable for damages and at risk of prosecution.

Cover watercolour painting of Talinga by Beryl Sinclair.

Published by Margaret Anne Sinclair with assistance from
Ignite & Write Publishing, www.igniteandwritepublishing.com

ISBN: 978-1-7640686-0-4 (pbk)   eISBN: 978-1-7640686-1-1 (ebook)

 A catalogue record for this book is available from the National Library of Australia

Foreword

This foreword is rather unusual, not so much because the present writer is the former spouse of the author, but for its composition before the completion of the book. This is due to the present writer's advanced age, which might cause him to miss the boat!

When Margaret first proposed that I should write the prologue to her book, I suggested the rather worn title *The Sinclair Saga*, having a first-hand knowledge of the family's history and travails. This suggestion was unceremoniously turned down by Margaret's pronouncement that *Talinga* was going to be the title. Having enjoyed for two weeks the majestic scenery from the Sinclair hearth on Eurong Beach in 1978, I quickly rested my case.

Margaret and I met in the Cardiac Intensive Care Unit of Baylor University Medical Center in July 1972. I was starting my third-year Fellowship in cardiac surgery and she was part of a group of vivacious, well-trained, well-groomed nurses from Down Under brought in to alleviate the nursing shortage. She stood out from the crowd with her upright stance, feline agility and a pair of mesmerising green eyes contrasting with her sun-tanned skin. Things moved fast, as the reader can understand, and a few months later she announced that she would be accompanying me back to Greece at the end of the academic year. To affect this, she trained as an open-heart perfusionist, a speciality missing from the university department where I was going to work. When there, she promptly delivered what was expected of her, at the same time setting up a Cardiac Intensive Care Unit by recruiting foreign nurses residing in Athens.

A year and a half later, in spite of what appeared progress, we both gloomily agreed that real change remained elusive. The mentality of the leadership was obsolete and the new generation of colleagues passive and compliant with the will of the establishment. It was then that Margaret took the initiative: "Let's get back to the States so you can work toward your certification as a fully-fledged American surgeon. I will back you up all the way!"

That she did over the next ten years in Boston, Richmond and London, England, as I was moving from general to cardiac surgery and then to transplantation. Margaret, working independently, went from one leadership position to another, eventually breaking into the traditionally conservative British system with her ingenious positioning mattresses for premature babies, which became later the nucleus of her business in the States.

Back in Dallas, in 1984, she put in long hours of arduous work in setting up her business without help, connections or capital. She was, at the same time, the inventor, the worker, the manager and even the courier delivering her products. She was named Business Person of the Year in 1989, only to see her labours fall into the abyss a year later when the Consumer Protection Agency shut down her business along with other similar enterprises, blaming their products for the not infrequent crib deaths in the community. Leaving aside the trauma of the unfair and arbitrary decision, we were left with a substantial debt. Undaunted, Margaret embarked on rebuilding the business with new products. She was again successful, that being her "finest hour", confirming the slogan of my teacher and mentor, Dwight E. Harken, the Father of Cardiac Surgery: "Good guys always bounce back".

This prologue would be incomplete if I did not pay tribute to Margaret's three seminal interventions in my career. I have already mentioned the first one about leaving Greece in 1974. She did it again four years later by helping me to make the transition from general to cardiac surgery. I was then literally exhausted after fifteen years of training and thus hesitant to embark on a new venture. She solved the problem by taking the bull by the horns and mailing the contract. The third one materialised when we were rather comfortably settled in London and the offer came from Baylor for me to start a Heart Transplantation Program from scratch. It was a hard call to make but Margaret again took the initiative: "Let's do it. Push yourself one last time. Think of your old dreams and ambitions. Let's go." Ten years and 230 transplants later, she again proved to be right.

I missed her father, Charles Prescott, a kind and universally adored man but I did meet Margaret's mother Beryl, vivacious and colourful, straight out of the pages of a Victorian novella. Talinga was her mansion where she lived surrounded by the paintings and embroideries she had created. Then it was John, the renowned conservationist, physically and morally erect, who instantly became one of my heroes. Chris, the army officer, took me to the War Museum in Canberra, where we spent the whole day absorbing photographs and artefacts. He looked to me like an Anzac officer from the Gallipoli campaign of 1915. Last but not least her sister Jennifer, with her gentle disposition and hospitality, reminded me of a bygone era of family tranquillity and happiness.

It is more than fifty years since that crucial encounter in Baylor Intensive Care Unit. Recently I came across an aphorism by that remarkable author, politician and U.S. ambassador to Italy, Claire Booth Luce: "A man has only one escape from his old self: to see a different self in the mirror of some woman's eyes". I was fortunate to see the self I was aspiring to be in Margaret's eyes. For that I will be forever grateful.

Peter A. Alivizatos, M.D., F.A.C.S.
Athens, November 2024
Founder of Cardiothoracic Transplantation at Baylor University Medical Center, Dallas, Texas and the Onassis Cardiac Surgery Center, Athens, Greece
www.peteralivizatos.com

Preface

This book's format and the story of Talinga are both unusual. Talinga was my home away from home for nearly five decades as I worked abroad, maintaining essential contact with my family in Australia.

My inspiration to write this book originated from my recognition that K'gari's World Heritage status might never have come to pass if my parents, Beryl and Charlie Sinclair, had not built Talinga at Eurong in 1964.

Every brick of Talinga, which means 'sand hill' in the language of the Indigenous Butchulla people, was handmade with sand and water from the island, mixed with concrete brought from the mainland. My siblings and I helped where possible, especially during my visits home from nursing school in Brisbane and Perth. Building Talinga on what was then known as Fraser Island was a labour of love, a testament to Dad's determination and vision.

The establishment of Talinga provided a base that enabled my brother John Sinclair to not only connect to the land and marvel at its unique beauty, but also to observe the adverse impacts of the international mining industry's operations on the island.

Talinga's location was strategically advantageous for John during his efforts to question the political establishment and fight for the island's protection. Because he had a base on the island, he had time to study the island's ecology and truly understand its uniqueness.

In the 1970s, Eurong had fewer than ten private residences, and only a few were occupied. Our parents made Talinga their permanent home in

1968. Vehicles on the beach were rare at the time and what was then known as Fraser Island had only just opened for tourism.

Talinga served occasionally as a meeting place for the Fraser Island Defenders Organisation (FIDO), which John founded, along with other essential guests who supported John's mission. Mum often provided shelter and hosted these visitors, which helped alleviate her solitude. Dad's knowledge of the island's layout also made him an invaluable pool of knowledge to anyone who visited.

For me, Talinga is more than a house; it symbolises connection. It connects us to the island, to each other and to the countless stories that have unfolded within its walls. It has also been my anchor and the place I keep returning to in order to feel grounded.

Since my early years in Maryborough, Queensland, I have lived and worked in four countries over forty-eight years. I never had a plan set out for my life. I leapt at opportunities as they presented themselves. It has led me into rewarding careers, lifelong friendships and the privilege of being surrounded by people who are doing groundbreaking work in their respective fields.

Even though I have spent much less time physically on the island than most of my relatives, no matter what I was doing or where I was in the world at any given time, a piece of my heart was always at Talinga. It will always be where my heart is.

As the eldest of Beryl and Charlie Sinclair's remaining children, at eighty-one years of age, I feel a profound responsibility to share my life story and our family's history with the island. These stories are not just ours, but are part of a larger narrative about resilience, love and the bond between people and place.

This memoir is my way of honouring that legacy, ensuring that the heart of the island continues to beat for future generations of people who visit.

Margaret

Contents

The Sinclair family	1
Growing up in Maryborough	7
Life as a nursing student	19
Land release at Eurong	23
Midwifery in Perth	31
Grand opening of tourism at Orchid Beach	37
Tutor sister at Royal Children's Hospital in Brisbane	47
A year of momentous events for the Sinclair family	55
Life in the USA	69
Cyclone Daisy strikes Talinga	77
Working in Athens	81
War in Cypress and a hasty escape to Australia	89
Back home at Talinga	95
The move from Greece to the USA	99
A new life in Boston	105
John's legacy	111
Essential personnel during the Boston Blizzard	115
From Boston to Richmond	119
Remembering Dad at Talinga	123
New concept in nurse scheduling	129
London calling	135
My first invention	145
Texans once more	149

My new life as an entrepreneur	153
Achieving goals	159
My farewell visit to Mum	167
The recall	175
Rising from the ashes	179
The Goldman Environmental Prize	189
Designing Masinali Originals	195
Peter's return to Greece	199
Soft Splint infringement	205
First attempt at retirement	209
JJ's arrival	213
The birth of Maggies	217
Alain's illness	221
Business growth	223
Final return to Australia	233
My connection to K'gari through Kingfisher Bay	241
Epilogue: A legacy of connection	243
About the author	249
References	251

The Sinclair family

Pre-1943

Before the name Sinclair became forever tied to K'gari, my family had a long-standing presence in Maryborough, Queensland. My great-grandfather Charles Sinclair was born on June 15, 1856, in Kent, United Kingdom, and my great-grandmother Annie Marie Claringbold, born in Dover six months later. They married in April 1876.

Charles I had immigrated to Australia at the age of twenty-eight at the request of the Queensland Government to work as an engineer at the newly established railway in Maryborough. Maryborough got its name from the Mary River, which had been named in honour of the wife of Governor Sir Charles Fitz Roy. It was proclaimed a town in 1861 when it was primarily a wool-shipping point. It became a city in 1905 and later developed as a marketing centre for a mixed farming region.

Charles arrived in Brisbane on *S.S. Buceleagh* in mid-June 1884. Within a month of arrival, he had qualified as a fireman and engine driver for the Queensland Railways. Three weeks after his arrival, he commenced driving in Maryborough on July 3, 1884.

At the time, he was separated from Annie Marie, but Charles gave 174 Tooley Street as his address when he sponsored his wife and family to immigrate.

Annie Marie travelled with their four children: Henry George (9), Louisa (8), Charles Arthur Sinclair (7), and Anna 'Kitty' (5). They boarded

SS Dacca, which left London on November 13, 1889. The ship arrived in Brisbane on January 6, 1890, and the journey took fifty-five days.

Charles and Annie Marie reunited after five years apart, and Alfred Prescott Sinclair was born in Maryborough in 1891, becoming their first Australian-born child. Charles prospered, and his position at the railway made him somewhat of a local legend. His nickname at the railway was 'Dover', and the family home affectionately became known as Dover Cottage.

Back then, a railway driver held a status similar to that of a jumbo jet pilot today. Coupled with his innate charm, my great-grandfather was well-respected around town.

My grandfather, Charles Arthur Sinclair, married Martha Clara Smith on June 4, 1906, at the Anglican Church Pialba. A year earlier, Clara's parents gave the newly engaged couple the money to build a new home at 71 Queen Street, Maryborough, where they lived happily for fifty-five years. Queen Street runs parallel to the Mary River and is separated only by a small floodplain.

Interestingly, Clara was born at 50 Queen Street, the home of the local midwife, Mrs Dow, on December 21, 1881. By coincidence, over eighty years later, after the old Dow home had been replaced, my brother John Sinclair purchased a house rebuilt on that site in 1964, and two of his sons were conceived there.

Clara had no formal vocational training, but she developed a talent for being a florist. She operated a small florist business, which she set up under her home on Queen Street. Her four daughters also developed talents as florists and developed small cottage industries together. Her oldest son Arthur opened a florist shop

Charles Sinclair, the first owner, who purchased the 1905 De Dion Bouton in 1914 from Dr. Garde of the Maryborough Base Hospital

in Adelaide Street, near the Central Hotel. The only family rift occurred when there was competition between mother and daughters over florist customs. Most of the flowers were grown in their home back garden, but Charles Arthur used to gather supplementary flowers for the business on his bicycle. The major business was preparing wreaths for funerals, bouquets for weddings, and corsages for special occasions.

In 1914, Charles I purchased the first automobile to come to Maryborough—a 1905 De Dion Bouton—which had previously been owned by Dr. Garde of the Maryborough Base Hospital.

Young Beryl in 1933

It is reported that this was his sole transport, and he used it to take his grandchildren for rides as a reward for being good. My father, Charles Prescott Sinclair, would have been among those grandchildren, as he was born on September 14, 1912, and he was said to have been a well-behaved young man.

My father, Charles Prescott, was a great sportsman in his youth. He rowed for Queensland in the King's Cup in Melbourne, played pennant-grade tennis, and had a record as a rugby league player at school. He attended the Maryborough Central State School and the Maryborough Grammar School, where he passed his Junior Public Examination.

Though born in different parts of Queensland, my father met my mother, Beryl Annie Vene Wilson, in 1933 when Mum was assigned as a teacher to work at the Albert State School in Maryborough. She had only been in town briefly before they met, and they were both twenty-one. My mother was born twenty-four hours before my father in 1912, Mum on September 13, and Dad on the 14th.

They were married on September 20, 1935. My parents honeymooned on Fraser Island, which has since been renamed K'gari. They stayed in a cabin at the newly opened Happy Valley Resort and arrived just two months after the *SS Maheno* ran aground that July.[1] *SS Maheno* was an ocean liner belonging to the Union Company of New Zealand that operated in the Tasman Sea, crossing between New Zealand and Australia from 1905 until 1935 before being converted into a hospital ship.

At the end of its commercial life, it was sold to a Japanese company and was being towed out of Sydney on July 3, 1935, by *The Oonah* on its way to Osaka when, four days later, the towline broke in a cyclone about fifty miles off the east coast of Queensland.

Attempts to re-attach the towline failed in the heavy seas, and the *Maheno*, with a skeleton crew of eight men aboard, drifted off. It was found beached off the coast of K'gari on July 10 and the crew had set up camp onshore to await assistance from *The Oonah*, which came two days later. The *Maheno* was unable to be refloated and the wreck has remained there ever since.

As kids we used to love looking at the black and white photos of my parents at Happy Valley. It looked like a magical, other–worldly place. The Happy Valley Resort closed soon after their stay due to the effects of the Great Depression.

Unfortunately, as was the law then, Mum was forced to abandon her promising teaching career once she became a married woman, though her future children certainly benefitted by having a qualified

Charles and Beryl Sinclair at their wedding in 1935

teacher at home fulltime. Beryl was a woman with the ability to perform to anything creative and excelled in cooking and cake decorating, knitting, sewing, smocking, crocheting, macrame, lamp making, gardening, landscaping, painting, writing, history, and interior decorating were just a few of her extraordinary talents.

St Paul's church in Maryborough

We were part of the Church of England congregation and Mum was heavily involved in the fundraising events, many of which would be themed.

She would transform the plain wooden-floored hall into a garden oasis complete with ponds and potted plants that would make you feel like you were in a secret garden. It was amazing what she could envision and create with the resources she had access to.

I guess her family had strong creative genes as one of her London-based cousins worked for Sir Norman Hartnell – a leading British fashion designer. Sir Hartnell gained the Royal Warrant as dressmaker to Queen Elizabeth (later the Queen Mother) in 1940 and Royal Warrant as dressmaker to Queen Elizabeth II in 1957.[2]

My great-grandmother Annie Marie died at the age of eighty on Christmas Day 1935, just one year and two days before her first great-grandson, my brother Noel Charles Sinclair, was born just a short distance from where they both lived. John Sinclair arrived shortly after on July 13, 1939.

According to a 2003 newspaper article, the Hecker family, who owned the Holden dealership when Charles died in 1941, purchased my great-grandfather's De Dion Bouton for ten pounds. Grandpa Sinclair, born in Dover, UK, in 1882, followed in his father's footsteps and became a railway engine driver for the Maryborough Railway. He held that position for almost forty years. He was a model of rectitude and virtue, and unlike his father, he had never driven an automobile. The De Dion automobile could not be

Margaret's great-grandfather Charles' stained glass window

passed on to him when my great-grandfather died, but he preferred his bicycle anyway.

Unfortunately, I did not meet either of my great-grandparents, but they lived on in the stories passed down through the generations. My great-grandfather died just two years before I was born. The original photo used by the newspaper reports of Charles was the very first one I had ever seen of him, as pictures those days were rare. Both of my great-grandparents, who had been prominent Maryborough citizens, have memorial stained-glass windows in the St. Paul's Church of England, ironically, it was right next door to Hecker Motors.

Margaret's great-grandmother Annie's stained glass window

Growing up in Maryborough

1943-59

I was seven years old when I had a near-death experience. I woke up in the night, and my nose was bleeding. Not wanting to wake anyone, I just held my head over the dish and let the blood drip. Fortunately for me, something woke my parents up and when they came to check on all of us, they found this dish full of blood with me looking dreadfully pale.

I was rushed to St Stephen's Hospital, and while I can remember Dad carrying me up the stairs, I was unconscious by the time we got inside. I was rushed to the operating room, where Dr. Ian Forbes, our very close friend, was waiting for us to arrive.

I vividly remember being outside my body, above the lights in the theatre, and watching the doctors at work. Mum told me when I was old enough to understand that I'd suffered a cardiac arrest. I'd lost so much blood that they had to give me a transfusion to replenish my body, but there was no time to crossmatch everything officially through the lab. Because I was on the brink of death, Dr. Forbes arranged for me to have a direct transfusion from the veins of the head of the lab into my own.

That decision saved my life.

I'd had an adenoidectomy a week before and this profuse bleeding was the result of a post-surgery haemorrhage.

My birthday was August 21, 1943, 100 years after the town was founded in 1843. By the time of my arrival, Maryborough was growing rapidly. The population of Maryborough in the 1947 Census was 14,395, and by 1966, it had grown to 19,659, a growth of 5,264 in 20 years.

However, this trend has reversed, and as I write this, growth has steadily declined, reducing the population to 15,287 by the 2021 Census.

Mary Hecker was named my godmother, and the same family owned the Holden dealership that had purchased my great-grandfather's De Dion. The Heckers are also synonymous with Maryborough. Mary's husband, Samuel William, was a renowned aviator and has been captured for posterity on a mural on Adelaide Street.

Sam was a foundation member and president of the Maryborough Aero Club. His historic 1928 Gipsy Moth was the first aircraft to fly under the Sydney Harbour Bridge and arrived in Maryborough in 1931. Sam was an associate of Sir Charles Kingsford Smith, who gave public joy flights in his famous *Southern Cross* from the Hecker property in New South Wales.

Margaret at seven months old with her dad

Sam had been a flying officer and aeronautics instructor in the RAAF and he competed in motorcycle, motor vehicle and aeroplane competitions for fun. Sam managed the General Motors Holden Dealership for fifty years and held official positions in many local organisations with active community involvement. His wife, Mary, just like my mother, was a socialite, and when they weren't raising their respective families, they were heavily involved in the community.

With two older brothers, Noel and John, and my two younger siblings, Jennifer and Chris, my father worked hard. He and my mother were always available to us, so we really flourished. We were all born while living on Queen Street—the same street my grandparents and several aunts and uncles lived on.

My father had a series of clerical jobs before being appointed the Texaco Oil Company depot keeper in Maryborough, a position he held until 1940. He was recruited to work in the Australian Army Petroleum Oils and Lubricants (POOL). Even though he never left his home or civilian job, he was credited with two years of active military service. He was required to supply fuel and oil to the district and service military convoys that passed through on their way to north Queensland. The army also commandeered Dad's Chevy utility for the war effort, which was his pride and joy.

Jennifer and Margaret, 1946

I don't remember these times, but John recalled the war years brought a lot of shortages, and any savings families had quickly evaporated. As a result, toys were a luxury we could not afford. John said two large toys our parents bought before the war became the only toys we didn't create ourselves. They were a wooden rocking horse and a metal pedal car. The rest, we improvised or were created by us from whatever materials we could find, so our imaginations were given a real workout.

My sister Jennifer was born on September 12, 1944, one year and three weeks after me. We were very close, and

Margaret and Jennifer, 1947

Mum was delighted that she had two girls to make clothes for after having two boys. She used her creative talents by making us matching outfits from delicate fabrics and using her smocking ability so she could show off her girls!

Jen had the most amazing head of hair, while mine was fine and took forever to grow. I was born very bald, and in fact, I had nothing for a long time. Dad used to shave my head to try and make it grow. My sister had much more luck with the hair gene and had full pigtails in no time, while I still had this thin, ratty hair. I wondered if I could borrow some of my sister's hair, so one day I took her behind the door with mum's scissors and cut off a pigtail. I was distraught when I couldn't attach it to mine, and I was really in trouble when Mum found out!

My young brother Chris Wilson Sinclair was born on August 23, 1946, and our family was complete. Chris was ten years junior to Noel, but he modelled himself after our oldest brother in many ways, even deciding to follow a similar career path as he got older.

Because our siblings were divided into two distinct age groups, my older brothers would often be off at school and get jobs while we were still young, so Jen, Chris, and I spent the most time together.

There were many times when we would get up to mischief together. One episode was when someone cut all the hairs off mum's hairbrush. It was clear that it was not John or Noel because they were much older than we were, but nobody ever found out which of the younger three was responsible for the crime on this particular day. It is a mystery that remains to this very day! Chris swears it wasn't him, Jennifer swears it wasn't her, and I know it wasn't me. Every time the three of us get together, even now, that's one of the things we still talk about. While it is ancient history, no one has confessed.

We moved from Queen Street to 264 Pallas Street in 1946. There was a lot of bush and paddocks to explore there. I suffered terribly from asthma, which I thankfully grew out of by the time I was fourteen. But until then, I was always affected when Dad would mow the lawn. When it was freshly mown, there were clippings all over the yard and my older brothers would pin me down and tickle me. I ended up with an asthma attack every single time from the combination of the grass and me laughing so hard. Mum would get so mad because the doctor would have to come over to administer some medicine so I could breathe properly again. Until the lawn was next mowed...

Dogs were a constant in our family life. The first I remember was Flicka. I forget what breed he was, but he had long hair. We were all playing under the house, which was one of our favourite places because, like all the Queenslanders of the time, the house was on stilts. There was nothing but compacted dirt under the house, so we chased each other around the posts and had a great time. Mum had decided to paint the house, and Flicka rolled in the green paint. We had to all pitch in to wash him to get it out of his fur.

~

After the war, Dad became a commercial traveller for Caltex from 1948 to 1951. This meant Dad got a company car, and it was so much nicer travelling with him in the sedan than it had been in his old ute, where we would lie on mattresses in the ute tray.

Looking back on my school report cards from my second year of primary school, I had a total of thirty-four days absent because of my adenoidectomy and the haemorrhage that followed. Still, as the terms progressed, my grades became better. At my school, they ranked students by capability and grades, and I went from seventh all the way up to second, which I was very proud of.

Noel, John, Margaret, Jennifer and Chris, 1947

As we got older, we would spend time with my grandparents, Martha Clara (nee Smith) and Charles Arthur Sinclair. My grandparents would drive us to Hervey Bay on weekends. You can get there in less than twenty minutes now, but it was a bit more of a drive back then. We created many memories in the harbourside town, but I remember the oak trees triggered my asthma and the doctor would always have to come around to give me an adrenaline shot to open up my airways again. One shot each time, and then I was okay.

Grandpa Sinclair was a churchwarden at St Paul's Anglican Church, but he was much more engaged than simply opening the church for services and functions. Twice a week for fifty years, he rode to visit the sick at Maryborough Base Hospital. This was a round trip of more than six miles on his two wheels.

He would cycle to visit friends and family, all of whom had been conditioned to save their old copies of the *Women's Weekly* and other magazines so he could deliver them to the hospital patients on his next visit.

When we weren't with my grandparents, my older brothers were put in charge of us younger three. There was many an unusual event that would occur when it was just the five of us kids at home. Wherever there was a twisted loaf—the most amazing bread—the boys would physically fight to see who would win to claim that sought-after morsel.

One day, John chased Noel through the house to get the twist, but Noel slammed the glass door shut behind him as he raced off. John's arm went through the glass panel, leaving his forearm partially attached to the severe gash. I'll never forget the flesh hanging and blood everywhere... lucky I had a strong stomach.

Not long after that incident, Mum decided she needed live-in help to supervise us while helping Dad with his business. Veronica was like a big sister to us. In her twenties, she understood our needs perfectly and gave Mum peace of mind that there was always at least one trustworthy person in the house. We all loved 'Vonnie', who lived with us for many years at Pallas Street.

Another vivid memory from our time on Pallas Street is when John brought a goat. When the car pulled up, he would welcome us with his "Baa".

Hence, he was dubbed Baaaa-zil, or simply Basil for those who didn't want to emphasise the sound.

John had been working at a nearby farm, and he decided to make some money by renting Basil out for animal husbandry. At that time, he would drive Dad's green 1929 Chevy. He took me with him to deliver Basil for a stay of duty across town. Basil was loaded into where the back seat had been located (John had removed it to provide a safe travelling 'compartment' for Basil), and off we went to somewhere in Granville. To get there, driving down the main street in town was necessary, and I was embarrassed. I felt the need to hide as I didn't want my school friends to see me, with Basil poking his head out of the back seat bellowing.

John always made a special effort to spend as much time as possible with his younger siblings before he had his own family. Although there was a four-year age gap between John and me, five with Jen, and seven with Chris, he gave us all he could of his time that was age-appropriate.

Dad ran Kann's Service Station on the corner of Walker and Tooley Streets, Maryborough, from 1951. We moved again from Pallas Street to 168 Tooley Street to be closer to the business Dad had bought. The house was right across the road, with a direct line of sight from our dining room table

Kahn's Garage circa 1963

to the garage, so even when Dad was home, he could keep an eye on the business. Noel was a brilliant student, but he spent most of his free time with Dad, helping out at the service station. John also helped out too.

As I've been looking back at my family history, I realised this home was two doors down from the one my great-grandfather had lived in when he first immigrated from England. I've passed that house countless times without realising its significance to our family.

Mum was an artistic person, and this extended to her landscaping pursuits, so all of our homes had the most beautiful gardens. In Tooley Street, Mum created the most incredible Japanese garden with a pool, an ornate lantern, and plants that made it look like it had come straight out of a postcard from Japan.

The De Dion was a piece of history

I finally got a pet of my own, a blue budgerigar that I called Nicky. I clipped one of his wings so he could escape his cage and wander free around the house without flying off. We had a dog called Cedric, who was another rescue; he was a funny old thing. I would leave Nicky's cage door open, and he would often hitch a ride on Cedric's back to move freely around the house.

His favourite thing was to go to what we called the breakfast room to see if Dad was in his favourite chair. Dad wore long socks, which created the perfect ladder for Nicky to climb. Once he ran out of socks, he would grip onto Dad's leg hairs to make it up to his shorts and continue on up to finally reach his shoulder.

Rather than sitting there like a regular bird, Nicky loved beer, and if Dad were having one, he would make his way down his arm and dip his head into the glass to drink with Dad. When the beer was freshly poured, his whole head would get covered in the froth, and he'd shake it off everywhere.

My hair was longer at that stage, and whenever I took Nicky out to run errands for Mum, he would sit on my shoulder and cuddle into the nape of my neck. I loved Nicky; he had a real personality. I was devastated when, after a few years, I went to get him out of the cage, and he was lying on his back with his feet up. It may have been a heart attack from too much beer...

There was a fire in Maryborough on November 6, 1956, and my great grandfather's De Dion was destroyed. The Hecker family had cared for the car as a real treasure and were determined not to lose such an essential piece of history. The family worked hard to restore her to her former glory, and I believe she is still in working order today, more than 120 years after she was manufactured.

My grandparents' golden wedding anniversary was a huge family occasion. In 1956, every child, grandchild, and great-grandchild attended celebrations in the Pialba Memorial Hall, along with all of those who had married into the family. There had not been a death in the family in those fifty years, which was another cause for celebration. There were forty-three of us in the extended family at that stage, most of whom lived in Maryborough.

～

Maryborough Central State School

School was never really difficult for me as I have a photographic memory. I shared a bedroom with my sister, and there would be times when Mum would come by to make sure we were studying. I'd hide a comic book inside the cover of a textbook because I didn't need to revise my notes, it was already in my head.

I wrote notes in class because we were expected to, but I never went back to them because it was a waste of time. I also found that I could remember things better if I simply listened to the teacher, as I could never write as fast as she talked anyway. If I wasn't actively listening, I might miss things.

I moved on to Maryborough Girls School for my secondary education. I chose a composite course for junior high school to get a mix of many different subjects. I had no idea that this course, which included English, math, bookkeeping, typing, dressmaking and cooking, would help me develop skills in every area I would work in professionally as an adult.

I liked it because the course offered practical skills, and even at that young age, I knew I would benefit from each one. Just as I had done in

Maryborough Girls School in 1958

primary school, I was an excellent student, with mostly As and only a couple of Bs on my final certificate.

The only blip on the radar for high school was a basketball injury I sustained in 1959 when I was about sixteen. But even this was an important milestone as it set my professional trajectory. I was sent to the hospital to have an x-ray on my wrist. While I was sitting in the waiting room, my mind wandered off to what I wanted to do with my life. It was all most parents were talking about at the time as I'd reached the age where I could leave high school to pursue a profession if I wanted to. The trouble was that I had no idea what I wanted to do.

Taking in the hustle and bustle of the doctors popping in and out of the waiting room and nurses tending to patients, I was lost in it when I thought *hmmm, that'd be a nice job.* When I was finally called in for my turn, I was moved to another waiting area for the x-ray machine and noticed a sign on an office door indicating the matron's office. Back then, the matron was the most senior nurse in a hospital. I knocked on the door, and Matron Finlay was at her desk.

"What do you have to do to become a nurse?" I enquired.

The matron knew my family well as she had filled up at our petrol station for years. She was delighted I was considering a career in nursing and told me I had to wait another year until I was seventeen before I could enrol as a trainee nurse.

"However, if you qualify..." she continued "... which I think you do because you get good results in school, you can become a cadet nurse at sixteen."

From that moment on, I knew *exactly* what I wanted to do. I seized the opportunity to get a head start and left school to become a cadet nurse on January 1, 1960, knowing that as soon as I turned seventeen, I would 'graduate' to student nurse.

Life as a nursing student

1960-63

Let me tell you, there was nothing glamorous about being a cadet nurse. Because I was too young to take on any 'real' work, I was responsible for scrubbing bedpans, taking and recording patients' temperatures with glass thermometers, making beds and giving sponge baths to bedridden patients.

I met my best friend, Gloria Hock, while we were both cadet nurses at the Maryborough Base Hospital. We were clocking up hands-on experience from our first day on the job, learning how to manage and interact with patients in

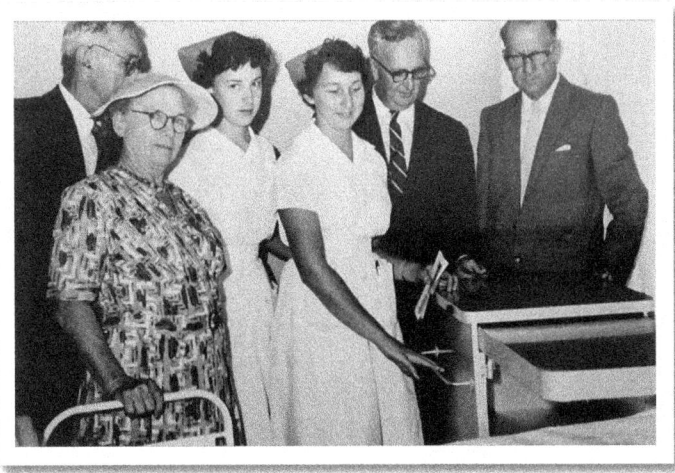

Cadet nurse Cynthia Lindaberg and me at the
Wahroonga Hospital grand opening

a way that made them feel safe and cared for. These foundational skills and the elbow grease I had to put in for those first eight months were the best possible foundations for my nursing career.

Because my birthday was in August, I moved up to student nurse four months before Gloria's birthday, which was in December. This meant I became a resident at the Nurses Quarters at the Maryborough Base Hospital, about a mile from the family residence, so I was constantly in touch with my parents.

I bought a motor scooter as my first mode of transport, which sparked a lifelong love of getting around on two wheels. Whenever I had a couple of days off at the same time as other friends, we'd head down to Hervey Bay to have parties and spend the night before coming back to work. Gloria would sometimes join me as my pillion passenger for these trips, and we always had a blast.

By the end of 1960, John celebrated his twenty-first birthday with our smallish family of seven. That same year, my first niece, Vicky, was born to Noel and his wife, Dalry 'Dal' Bray, whom he had married two years earlier.

Noel and Dal's wedding day, 1958

LIFE AS A NURSING STUDENT

The Sinclair family at John's 21st birthday, 1960

Although Noel was seven years my senior, I adored him. He was amazingly active and always out with his friends. He was the first in the family to drive and took us out for drives as soon as he got his licence.

We also celebrated Chris reaching his scholarship year at high school.

Grandpa Sinclair died on January 13, 1961. I don't ever remember him being ill because he had a heart attack and died quite suddenly. I was in my second year of nursing when he sadly passed away.

While Noel had begun a career in the military, John dove into agriculture, and I was training to become a nurse, Jennifer followed in Mum's footsteps and started at the Teachers Training College at Kedron, Brisbane, in 1962.

John and Helen Lane married in Brisbane in 1962 when I was nineteen.

Grandpa and Grandma Sinclair, 1956

Land release at Eurong

1963-64

Around the age of ten, Dad introduced me to the magnificent K'gari. We would stay at Happy Valley in a primitive tin hut with enough bunk beds to accommodate us all. Dad would put a pipe into the sand to extract water from the dune lakes, one of the features that made K'gari unique.

The island has around forty freshwater lakes, most above sea level and higher than where the tin hut sat. The pipe would provide us with ample drinking water and the ability to have showers on the beach. Back then, there were no cars on the beach and very little other human activity, so we could run around without clothes on and no care in the world.

In my teenage years, we'd be able to take friends over to hang out with, and there were always magical times to be had. The families who regularly holidayed on K'gari came to know each other very well. One of the most prominent men in personality and physical presence was a fisherman named Sid Melksham, who became a pioneer for

Margaret (right) with school friends at Happy Valley, 1956

TALINGA

Four generations of Sinclairs, 1963

Dal, Noel and their children, 1963

The Sinclair siblings at Christmas, 1963

local tourism after he developed the Eurong Beach Resort and established Fraser Island's Ferry Service.

It wasn't until September 6, 1963, that my father purchased Allotment No 9, Section 3 in Eurong, Area 25.6 Perches from the Burrum Shire and the Maryborough Land Agent's District. It was to be the family's slice of the K'gari paradise. He had unsuccessfully tried to secure land at Poyungan Valley, but the public auction saw him secure the best block in Eurong at the public auction.

Later that year, Chris and his friend Brian Watts travelled to the island to establish a base for the recently acquired land. Together, they built a one-room, prefabricated hut with two folding beds, which was to become the staging point for the construction of Talinga.

The little hut provided my wonderful first memories of an outdoor 'dunny' with the most spectacular beach view. It was also a happy home for toads, snakes, and lots of march flies—huge flies that liked to bite you if you weren't quick enough to swat them away. Nevertheless, it was heaven, and I remember going there every opportunity I had to check out the progress.

On November 22, 1963, I was back at home as usual on my days off, when Dad woke me up at four in the morning. He looked ashen as he handed me a cup of tea and informed me that American President John F. Kennedy had been Assassinated in Dallas, Texas. I will never forget that moment. I don't remember knowing much, if anything, about Dallas then, and never in a million years did I think it would ultimately become the city where I was destined to live more than half my life.

I completed my third year of nursing training at Maryborough Base Hospital in December.

The practical training had been the perfect grounding for me. There were some challenging moments, like when we had to watch a postmortem examination. I went to the morgue, and a policeman and several other nursing students had to be present for official reporting. The forensic pathologist, who had to complete the autopsy and report to the coroner for the cause of death, performed a craniotomy. This involved cutting into the skull and removing part of it to expose the brain. At one point, one of the policemen watching with us fainted and had to be revived.

It was confronting, to be sure, but equally fascinating. Now, I was living in the nurses' quarters, and they served fried brains for dinner that night. I quite enjoyed crumbed brains in those days; we had them a lot for family meals at home. But it was rather off-putting to have that particular delicacy presented on a plate for dinner that night, so I skipped it. I don't know that I ever had brains again.

The year of 1963 was the last Christmas I had with my family for many years to come, and it was great to share it with all four generations of Sinclairs, even though there were only fifteen of us then. We gathered for a meal in the backyard of our Tooley Street home. Chris was the only one living at home at that time, though Noel and John weren't far across the town.

While living in Maryborough, Noel's family had grown to six, with Greg, Russell and Danny joining their eldest, Vicky. They were the only grandchildren until John's firstborn, John Jr., arrived. John and Helen also welcomed Andrew and Keith in the following years, and Noel's youngest, Fiona, completed their family.

∽

I was twenty-one when I moved from Maryborough in 1964 to complete my final year of training in Brisbane. I spent most of the year in between the Princess Alexandra Hospital and the Royal Brisbane Children's Hospital.

I loved working with sick children, and at that time, it was so rewarding to see some of the sickest kids respond to their therapy and return to normal health. It was always a joyous occasion when they were finally ready for discharge. Of course, some didn't make it home, and these were the awful moments we had to deal with alongside their families.

Our group of student nurses had so much fun. When I think back to my days at Princess Alexandra Hospital, it's impossible not to smile at some of the escapades we got up to. Those were formative years—a whirlwind

Margaret, Charles and Beryl at Margaret's 21st birthday, 1964

of studying, working and bonding with fellow students, nurses and medical trainees. But it wasn't all serious. We knew how to have fun and nothing illustrates that better than the infamous Mad Mod Med Party.

It all started when a house across the street from the hospital became vacant. Someone had just moved out, and it sat there, empty and inviting. I don't know what came over me, but I saw an opportunity. "Let's have a party," I said, already buzzing with ideas. And so, I got to work organising what turned out to be one of the most memorable nights of my life.

We decided to transform the house into a mock hospital experience. Each room had a theme. Guests entered through the 'admissions room,' where they were 'processed' and ushered into the 'examination room'—no forms, no triage—just fun. IV drips were rigged up, but instead of saline, they dispensed liquor. It was cheeky, absurd and hilariously fitting for a group of medical trainees.

I can't recall all the details, but the premise was simple: laughter and good spirits.

Jennifer and Margaret at Margaret's 21st birthday

TALINGA

People mingled, danced and let loose as the house filled with music and chatter. The party raged on until the early hours. Around three o'clock in the morning, the police showed up to tell us to cut down the noise. But here's the kicker—instead of shutting us down, they joined in for a bit. After all, it was hard to resist the charm of a house full of young, carefree nurses and doctors-in-training.

Looking back, it feels like a snapshot from another lifetime. The year was 1965, and life felt more uncomplicated and unrestrained. That house on Ipswich Road symbolised our camaraderie and ability to find joy even amid the pressures of medical training. It wasn't just a party; it was a celebration of youth, shared dreams, and the enduring human spirit.

Sometimes, the most enduring memories are made when we let our hair down and embrace the sheer absurdity of life. The Mad Mod Med Party will always be one of those special moments.

I completed my time at Princess Alexandra Hospital at the end of 1964, and I was very proud to have my parents come to Brisbane for my graduation.

After graduating, I spent some time with my parents. According to Mum's meticulous diary, the actual building of Talinga did not start until that year, specifically on December 30, 1964.

Margaret with a patient at the Royal Brisbane Children's Hospital

Margaret's graduation with her Mum and Dad, 1964

Talinga at its lockable first stage in March 1965

Dad began to make bricks for the new house, using sand from the pristine beach and mixing it with powdered concrete to mould into bricks.

Within two weeks, by the end of January 1965, the house had lockable doors. While Dad laboured, Mum spent her time painting and decorating as the house came to life. Seven days later, it was painted inside and out. The house was quite small, with two rooms on the upper level.

Although my parents still lived and worked in Maryborough, they spent most weekends on the island. Mum would have been fifty-three years old at that time, and when she started something, she would not stop until she achieved the desired result. Knowing Mum, she enjoyed the time alone in the house to give it her unique personality.

Those early days at Talinga were so much fun. Only a few houses were built there, and we would do lots of party hopping. Muir Daniels and his wife Jan had an A-frame, and Sid Melksham also had two A-frames on his land, close to Talinga.

Chris earned a three-year scholarship to the Royal Military College Duntroon from 1965 to 1968 and was off to Canberra to complete his training.

Midwifery in Perth

1965-68

I'd kept in touch with Gloria, who had stayed on in Maryborough to complete her fourth year. Once we'd both graduated, I coerced her to join me for one year of midwifery training at the King Edward Memorial Hospital in Perth. I shocked her with the suggestion, as none of our other friends had travelled outside Queensland.

Going somewhere new and having some new experiences would be exciting. After being accepted, I arranged transportation to Perth and thought it would be more fun to go there by ship. So, I found a cruise ship called the *SS Marconi*, which went from Sydney to Perth, with a stop in Adelaide. After it dropped us off at the Freemantle Port, it would sail to the Mediterranean.

I thought that would be an exciting way for us to get there after a week in Sydney babysitting for Dr. Gerry Locke, one of Dad's close fishing friends. The Lockes had become family to me.

It was rough crossing the Great Australian Bight after we left Sydney in March 1965. The Marconi was a brand-new ship, and there was a lot of pomp and ceremony, with streamers flowing as we

Margaret and Gloria

Newspaper clipping of Margaret and Gloria's move to Perth

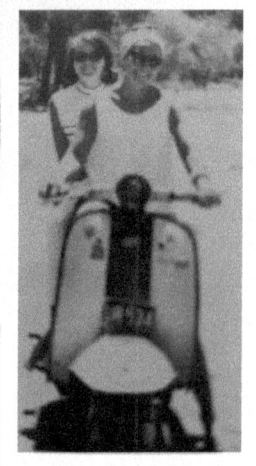

Maragaret and Gloria on the new scooter in Perth

pulled away from the Sydney dock. Many passengers could not find their sea legs and were ill for most of the journey. Fortunately, I was one of the few who never seemed seasick.

When we arrived at King Edward Memorial Hospital to report for training, Gloria and I were the only nurses from Queensland, while the rest were from all over Perth, Sydney and Melbourne. It was a massive move for two young ladies from Maryborough.

Of course, the first thing I had to do in Perth was find transportation. Having had a scooter while in Queensland, I didn't hesitate to find myself a used one and settled on a Vespa to enable us to get to and from the fabulous beaches.

Perth was a great place to live and work. Unfortunately, I had very little time to travel. The climate was quite different from that in Queensland—it was scorching, so hot and dry that you could fry an egg on the pavement! There was very low humidity in summer, and much colder than I had ever experienced in the winter.

For the very first time in my life, I had to get myself a coat, so I needed a sewing machine to make one. I still hadn't lost my interest in designing and making clothes, though I had little need for many civilian clothes as we wore uniforms provided by the hospital. Mum taught me how to sew when I was five, and I'd made my first skirt by the time I was six.

I remember the trendy white faux leather one I designed with an exciting collar resembling a polo neck and a full-length zipper.

Not long after my midwifery training began in 1966, the Australian Government rolled out the conversion from imperial to metric measurement. The hospitals were among the first to be impacted by the change, which necessitated the weighing of babies in kilograms and grams, all the IVs and fluids to be measured in litres and millilitres, and heights and lengths in metres and centimetres instead of feet and inches. This change greatly impacted the nursing staff, but we adapted surprisingly well.

After graduating from King Edward, I received my Midwifery Certificate. While Gloria returned home to Maryborough, I visited my parents at K'gari and then returned to Perth for a six-month Postgraduate Paediatric Course at the Princess Margaret Hospital.

Living in the nurse's quarters was enjoyable, and I had plenty of opportunities to attend parties. Apart from the work and the wonderful people I was working with, I also had the chance to go twilight sailing on the Swan River on many occasions with a young real estate agent named Alan Bond, who always had plans for an after-party.

~

With three nursing certificates—a four-year General Nursing, one year in Midwifery, and an additional six months in Postgraduate Paediatrics—I spent time between courses visiting my family before returning to Perth to work at the Hollywood Repatriation Hospital with geriatric patients. I enjoyed working with older people, even those who were deemed to be 'senile', and they were usually a pleasure to be around. Of course, it came with a unique set of challenges, but any specialist area of health care does.

TALINGA

Talinga, 1966

In December 1966, while living in the nurse's quarters at the Hollywood Hospital, a friend suggested we drive around Perth in my new Volkswagen Bug to see the Christmas lights. While I stopped at a red light and waited for the lights to change, another car ran at high speed into the rear of my vehicle.

I was shocked and unable to walk, so I was hospitalised and diagnosed with a neurogenic (paralysed) bladder. This happens when your spinal cord is damaged, causing a disruption of the nerves to the bladder. It causes an inability to urinate until the nerves regenerate over time and can recommence their usual function. I had to be catheterised every four hours while in hospital. Once I was released, I had to do it for myself for a few weeks until the nerve damage healed.

While still in the hospital, I was visited by an attorney who said he could get a cash settlement for my injury. I think the fellow who'd hit me had been a well-known person with some deep pockets, not that I cared about that; I was more focused on my health. The attorney promised to be in touch and went on his merry way, but I never thought any more about it.

I took a few weeks off work to visit my family and spend time with my parents at Talinga. They were still living full-time at 168 Tooley Street, and they cherished every opportunity to visit the island. For me, Talinga was the only place I went to for holidays, and I felt very fortunate to have such an amazing place to call home. There were still no neighbours, and the beaches were peaceful and free of vehicles and people.

~

While still working at the Repatriation Hospital, I went shopping to get a swimsuit one day, and I couldn't find anything I liked. The style of the time was low-cut legs that didn't suit my body. On the night shift one night, all the patients were settled, and I had to find something to do to keep myself awake, so I came up with a design that allowed maximum exposure to the sun without leaving strap marks. It was a two-piece connected in front, leaving the back open to the sun. There was no sunscreen back then, so we only used coconut or olive oils to protect our skin. I was so excited by this design that from the moment I got off duty at seven in the morning, I waited impatiently for the shops to open so I could buy some fabric. It was difficult to find elastic-type fabrics back then, so I had to settle for a stretch polyester.

Given my early foray into sewing, coupled with the sewing course that made up my high school certificate, I had plenty of tricks up my sleeve to bring my design to life. I had made the swimsuit by the time my next night shift started. Looking back, this design was ahead of its time and a little risqué for the era!

Several years later, after I returned to Queensland, I decided to get an opinion from a well-known swimsuit retailer on the Gold Coast. I took my designs to Paula Stafford, a designer credited with introducing the bikini to

Margaret's swimsuit design, 1966

Margaret and Gloria in swimsuits designed by Margaret, 1986

Australia in the early 1950s, to see if it was something she could produce for her label.[3] While it wasn't for her, I was offered a job as a designer for the swimwear brand Jantzen, but I declined as I loved nursing too much. It was apparent quickly that the design industry was cut-throat, so I decided to shelve my design inclination until I had the finances to set up my own company. Little did I know then that opportunity would present itself again some 30 years later.

~

Chris' Duntroon Graduation, 1968

The year 1968 was an exciting time for the family when Chris graduated from Duntroon in Canberra as a Lieutenant in the Royal Australian Infantry, and I completed my pediatrics course in Perth.

I had time off at the same time as Chris and we were able to spend time at Talinga together. While we were there, he had a bunch of his mates with him and it was fun taking care of the meals together.

We had massive rain for almost the entire time we were there, and with the rain coming down cats and dogs, it was hard to go outside to use the dunny on the hill without kicking the giant pesky cane toads! Needless to say, we spent most of our time waiting for a break in the weather, around the table playing Crib and Scrabble, with little to no contact on the mainland.

Grand opening of tourism at Orchid Beach

1968-69

Dad had left his post at the service station in 1968, and they had moved everything over from Tooley Street. It had been a long time coming as Dad, who had bowed legs, had been suffering terribly from being on his feet for long hours over many years. The condition had caused arthritis in his knees, and it reached the point where the only surface he could walk on without being in pain was sand.

It was the perfect time for them to move over to the island. Mum eagerly furnished the patio, so she was at home in her favourite role of entertaining and appropriately decorating her castle with loot she had salvaged on her beach walks.

One of the most memorable pieces of furniture they took with them is the table that had been our informal dining table.

Talinga, 1968

To this day, it has continued to be the most important gathering place for all members of the family.

Soon after my parents settled at Talinga, Sir Reginald and Lady Maureen Barnewall invited them to go to Orchid Beach to be assistant resort managers and prepare for the grand opening of the new Orchid Beach Resort. Because the resort was sixty miles away from Talinga, John took over responsibility for managing Talinga and renting it out in their absence.

Sir Reginald was a descendant of Anglo-Norman knights and the founder of Polynesian Airlines. During World War II, he served in Papua New Guinea (PNG) as a lieutenant with the Royal Australian Engineers and Z Special Unit AIF. After the war, he flew around many parts of PNG with Mandated Airlines. Sir Reginald founded Goulburn Valley Air Services (later called

A beach picnic in front of Talinga, 1968

Beryl holding court at Talinga, 1968

GRAND OPENING OF TOURISM AT ORCHID BEACH

Beryl, Charles, Noel and family, 1968

Southern Airlines Ltd) in 1954, servicing Victoria and Tasmania, including King and Flinders islands.

Having visited Apia in Western Samoa, Sir Reginald and his first wife decided to embark on a new tropical lifestyle and made it their new home. He quickly identified the need for a local airline to connect Apia with neighbouring Pago Pago in American Samoa. He founded Polynesian Airlines Ltd in 1959 with a Percival Prince ten-seater aircraft.

Sir Reginald obtained the lease of Orchid Beach from the Lands Department, and work began almost immediately at the resort. The first things to be constructed were the airstrip and two 'anglers lodges' as the Barnewalls wanted to create a self-catering fly-in, fly-out holiday option for anglers. Smaller units came later to be able to cater for self-catering visitors.

Due to the steep and loose surface at Middle Rocks, it was virtually impossible to reach Orchid Beach by traditional methods. Everything needed to build the lodges and units was taken from Maryborough to Wathumba Creek and then trucked across the island. The trip from Eurong to Orchid Beach by road takes around four hours and is 96 km.

Much of the freight was carried by Sid Melksham in the 'Lady Fraser', a boat he had salvaged from the bottom of the Burnett River.

Sir Reginald's time in Samoa inspired the redevelopment of the Orchid Beach site from a collection of self-contained lodges to a resort featuring buildings based on the shape of the Samoan *fales*. He also constructed a pool and central *phono fale*.

Mum contributed significantly to the decoration of the guest suites, and her craft skills ensured that each lodge and unit was impeccable.

Still, because no environmental impact study had been completed, half of the land between the buildings and the sea was swept away by natural erosion and cyclone activity over the years.

John, Helen and his two young sons flew from Maryborough to K'gari to visit Mum and Dad at Orchid Beach before continuing to Eurong. It was the first time John could see the island from the sky and appreciate the pureness of the landscape.

John had been maintaining Talinga for our parents. During that trip, he organised the first Fraser Island Safari for the members of the Maryborough and Bundaberg Wildlife Preservation Society. These safaris would later become key fundraising initiatives for his endeavours to protect the island from mining and logging.

Building the *phono fale* at Orchid Beach

Hearing that I was on leave from Repatriation Hospital, Sir Reginald invited me to come to Orchid Beach to be the 'island nurse'. This entailed looking after their son Joey, who had some health issues and needed regular injections.

I spent my time before the grand opening, helping out where needed around the resort, patching up cuts and administering immunisations to people so they didn't have to go to the mainland for treatment. The Barnewalls had constructed a rudimentary airstrip by the resort for guests

GRAND OPENING OF TOURISM AT ORCHID BEACH

Getting the drum — the Wright way

★ WHEN SENATOR REGINALD CHARLES WRIGHT, of Hobart, was appointed Minister in Charge of Tourist Activities in the Gorton Government, in 1968, one wry comment said the job should suit him because he "liked to get around."

This reference to the nimble-witted barrister from Hobart — a lecturer in law at the University of Tasmania and counsel for the university in the famous Orr case of 1956 — was an allusion to Senator Wright's "rebel" reputation: in the course of his parliamentary career he has many times crossed the floor to vote with the Opposition when he has disagreed with his party's line.

Now his Tourist Activities portfolio gets him around far from Canberra. When the Orchid Beach Island Village on Fraser Island (Q) was opened a few weeks ago, the effervescent Tasmanian was there to perform the ceremony — and to take a lesson from hostess Margaret Sinclair in how to beat the "lale."

The lale drum, from Samoa, is a hollow log that gives out a booming sound with extraordinary carrying power. At Orchid Beach it stands-in for a dinner gong.

Media coverage of the Orchid Beach opening

Margaret with Senator Wright

Orchid Beach transport

Orchid Beach staff on opening day

to have easy access, and it was so peaceful to lie on the 'runway' at night, looking up at the Milky Way and other constellations in the pristine sky. There were no lights, so it was my magic spot to view the stars and reflect as often as possible.

On evenings when I felt a little more energetic, it was fun to take a torch down to the beach and chase the soldier crabs.

Senator Wright officially opened the Orchid Beach Resort and designated Fraser Island a tourist destination.

On May 5, 1969, Grandma Sinclair died at eighty-eight. Grandpa and Grandma Sinclair's home on the corner of Queen Street and John Lane had been the location for family Sunday meals for decades. My memories of Grandma's house are of her amazing Sunday dinners, which seemed like a feast when all the cousins and families would gather at the table. Later, she would always hold court under the fragrant frangipani tree in the backyard.

Queen Street was where five generations of the Sinclair family were conceived, born, resided, or died. Every member of Clara and Charles II's family, except Florence, lived in Queen Street for at least a year or two after marriage. At the same time, several grandchildren also lived there after marriage.

In 1969, not long after returning from Orchid Beach, while working as a tutor sister in paediatrics at the children's hospital, I was admitted to the Royal Brisbane Hospital after contracting encephalitis. There were

This 2019 photo shows the home my grandparents lived in since it was built in 1906

many times when I'd been 'eaten alive' by mosquitos on the island. Just before I left the island, I woke up one morning to find sprinkles of blood all over the sheets from mosquito-bite wounds. Encephalitis is no joke; it is inflammation of the brain, and I was unconscious for a couple of days in the hospital. I was administered medication to reduce the inflammation and bring everything back under control.

Charles Sinclair, 1968

The hospital called Mum, who dropped what she was doing at Talinga and dutifully visited me. Fortunately, I had been treated early enough that I had no lasting after effects other than some memory loss.

After they departed from Orchid Beach, Mum and Dad moved to live full-time in Talinga; a few days later, on Sunday, July 20, they listened to the Apollo 11 moon landing on the radio with Sandy Luck from the comfort of Talinga. Dad was a huge fan of President John F. Kennedy, so he was proud to see this historic achievement come to pass. The late president had set this goal in motion six years before Americans could even orbit the Earth.

Neil Armstrong and Buzz Aldrin's transmissions were heard in a crackling transmission over the radio, and Neil's words, "The Eagle has landed," became immortalised.

Charles and Beryl at Talinga, 1968

My parents drove back to Orchid Beach to tender their resignations the day after the moon landing. Unable to fully retire, Dad started work as a storeman at Ungowa, the centre of the Forestry Island administration, on July 28, 1969. Because Ungowa was a challenging forty-five-minute drive from Eurong, Dad remained in the barracks during the week.

Although my parents didn't see much of one another, they made up for it when the weekends came, hosting endless parties with the slowly growing number of locals and visitors.

∼

GRAND OPENING OF TOURISM AT ORCHID BEACH

Chris had joined 8RAR at Enoggera in Queensland. His battalion arrived in South Vietnam on November 17, 1969, relieving 9RAR on November 25. The battalion formed part of the 1st Australian Task Force (1ATF) with 5RAR and 6RAR. It was based at Nui Dat, Phuoc Tuy province.

Less than a month after Chris' battalion arrived in Vietnam, my parents received an urgent telegram:

> It is learned with regret that your son, 17145 Lieutenant Chris Wilson Sinclair, sustained a superficial fragment wound to the left forehead on 14th December 1969, N.P.H Hoc Tuy Province Vietnam, and was admitted to 1 Australian Field Hospital Vung Tau Vietnam. If his condition remains satisfactory, no progress report will be forwarded to you.
>
> Signed
> Army Headquarters

This was followed shortly after by a handwritten letter from Chris on an Australian Red Cross letterhead. He said he felt "damned embarrassed" being in hospital after the incident, which he said saw him receive "a bit of "shrap" from a grenade (about quarter size of a threepenny bit) in the head about two inches above the left eye."

> *It was ridiculous. We didn't even see Charlie. He walked up, saw our sentry, fired several shots and left rapidly. Our fellas opened fire, and in fact, I was hurt by one of our grenades.*

Life was finally what my parents wanted: to be at their castle with all their worldly possessions and without the encumbrance of the home in Tooley Street. However, the sale did not go through as expected, which meant they were not yet free to make the improvements and finish Talinga as they wanted.

After being discharged from the hospital, I returned to Brisbane, and for the first time in my life, I had the honour of being a bridesmaid. It was for my dear friend Gloria. We had done all our nursing training together, and after Gloria left Perth, she returned to Maryborough and met John Hynes, a resident doctor at Maryborough Base Hospital.

They were married on December 15, 1969.

Margaret (second from left) as bridesmaid for Gloria and John Hynes, 1969

Tutor sister at Royal Children's Hospital in Brisbane

1970

I became a tutor sister at the Royal Children's Hospital and was there for about six months into 1970. We had a graduation ball for all the doctors and nurses, and I met a man called Bruce a couple of months earlier. Although he was much older than me, he seemed nice enough, and I invited him to be my partner at the ball. We were a few champagnes in and having fun on the dance floor when Bruce leaned over and said, "You know, we should get married".

I laughed and jokingly replied, "Oh, Bruce, that's a great idea!" I thought it was a joke as we hadn't known each other for so long. I excused myself to go to the bathroom, and when I came back into the room, the band stopped playing, and the singer cleared his throat.

"We have an announcement to make. Well, folks, one of our sisters, Margaret, and Mr Bruce have become engaged!" I almost died. All my nursing students were coming up and congratulating me. Some asked to see my ring, which I didn't have, so I made an excuse: "It was all such a surprise; I only just found out myself!"

Before I had much of a chance to process anything, Bruce contacted my parents at Talinga the next day and told them we'd decided to get engaged. Bear in mind that Mum and Dad had no idea this man existed. Let me tell you, there was no way I would get married and give away my career. I didn't want anything to do with him, let alone to be married to him. He was a convenient partner for the ball, but it still took a few months to clear Bruce and the phony engagement he had surreptitiously arranged.

My parents wanted to meet this man who was unexpectedly going to become part of the family, and Bruce brought along his friend Ray McDonald, whom my sister Jen fell in love with. So, at least something great came out of having an accidental fiancé!

On May Day, the weekend of 1970, I visited Talinga with my friend Barbara Craig and gave Mum a radio with a cassette tape recorder. The recorder was for Mum to send taped messages to Chris, who was on leave in Hong Kong. Later, she would use it many times to communicate with me while I was living on the other side of the world… but even I didn't know that was on the horizon for me at the time.

Mum also planted lawn turf in her newly established garden after the completion of the Talinga expansion. Before being declared a Tourist Island

Collin Smith and Melva on the beach with their vehicle alongside Charles and Pundi, 1976

A proud Charles with his new International Scout, 1970

in 1969 by Senator Wright at the opening of the Orchid Beach Resort, it was pretty uncommon to see many cars on the beach at all, and those residents who lived there knew that anything other than four-wheel drive vehicles was just a disaster waiting to happen.

Thankfully, Mum's sister Melva and brother-in-law Collin Smith had an uneventful drive when they came up from Brisbane to be greeted on the beach by Mum, Dad and Pundi.

Unfortunately, just a few months after the island was officially opened for tourists, seven people died, and many others were injured when a blitz wagon carrying forty-seven tourists rolled over after leaving Lake McKenzie.[4]

This tragedy occurred on July 22, 1970, when the only vehicles available as tourist buses were old Blitzes used in World War II.

On Wednesday, August 12, 1970, Dad and Noel went to the Land Sale in Maryborough and purchased additional land adjoining Talinga for $600. Jen built a home on the property adjacent to Talinga, and Mum named it Weeroona; the resting place. When the sign was made, it was misspelled, and from that day forward, it became known as Weerona.

I received a cheque in the mail as a settlement for my injuries in the Perth car accident. It was for $10,000, which was a lot of money in those days. I knew exactly what to do with the money—Dad needed a new four-wheel drive on the island as his old vehicle was rusted out and no longer able to be driven.

While staying with Mum in Maryborough on August 19, I went to Heckers Motors and put a $500 deposit on a used International Scout for Dad's upcoming birthday and Father's Day. Bruce and Ray checked it out, and both found it to be in excellent condition. The Scout was an off-road vehicle produced by International Harvester and featured a fold-down windshield. Dad took possession of it on August 31, following a weekend in Bundaberg with Noel, Dal, and the grandchildren. It was a vehicle that did not turn out to be a great choice for the island. Though it was in excellent mechanical condition, the body rapidly deteriorated with rust.

I bought the car and used the "easy come, easy go" settlement money on a cruise overseas.

I bought my first passport and booked a roundtrip cruise on the *SS Marco Polo*. The journey set off on October 8 and went from Brisbane to Singapore, Bangkok, Hong Kong, Manila and Port Moresby before returning to Brisbane. This trip may have triggered my urge to see the world one day. The second officer on that ship, Tony, really looked after me. He was British and a real gentleman, seating me at the captain's table for meals every night and introducing me to many amazing people. I seemed to be the only young single person on the ship, so I had all these older people looking after me for the entire cruise. While in Bangkok, I took the opportunity to purchase Thai silk in ivory, gold, and green for Jen's upcoming wedding to Ray in Easter 1971.

～

The first unit of Australian troops to be withdrawn from the Vietnam War and not replaced were the Brisbane-based B Company of the 8th Battalion of the Royal Australian Regiment (8 RAR). Their return to Brisbane in 1970 signified the beginning of Australia's disengagement from the war in Vietnam.

8RAR arrived at Hamilton Wharf on November 12, 1970. Chris' return home was a huge relief for our family.

One of their most significant operations was *Operation Hammersley*. This month-long mission ran from February 10 to March 9, focusing on reconnaissance in the Long Hai area. Eight days in, the battalion stumbled upon an enemy bunker system that had been abandoned after air raids.

They focused on patrolling the area for the rest of the operation, mainly using ambush tactics. These ambushes were highly effective and relatively low-risk—no small feat in such a volatile environment. For their involvement in Hammersley, the battalion earned the Meritorious Unit Commendation and the Cross of Gallantry with Palm Unit Citation from the South Vietnamese government.

Throughout their deployment, 8RAR was primarily involved in pacification efforts in Phuoc Tuy Province.

Soon after the boys had settled back on home soil, several made a pilgrimage to Eurong, which Chris had not seen for some time. By then, Eurong had developed considerably, but there were still no paved roads and vehicles had to drive on the soft sand tracks.

Sid Melksham had erected two A-frame buildings, one of which became the first store on the island in the early 1970s. The store sold very few necessities. Residents used their two-way radio to call an order, delivered by plane and landed in front of the house on the beach, just a few steps from Talinga.

Chris and the Duntroon boys after Vietnam, 1971

Sid's other A-Frame was the only accommodation available for guests on the island then. Most visitors were there on FIDO-related visits, as there were very few tourists on the island at that time. Sid's guests often became neighbourly friends with Mum, who was usually happy to have company while Dad was away with his forestry job.

According to Mum's handwritten diary, these were the houses built at Eurong in order of construction:

Houses built at EURONG June 1, 1970

1. Bob Oldfield
2. Sid Melksham (2 A-Frames)
3. Easton & Anderson
4. Williams
5. Sinclair
6. Jarvis
7. Kuhneman
8. Buffey
9. Daniels
10. Manton
11. Roper
12. Murdoch
13. Goodwin
14. McLardy

Chris with his buddies in Eurong

There was much excitement when the Instant 8 Block Machine arrived in December 1970. It allowed the family to get stuck into creating bricks to construct the next extension of the house. Each brick had previously been crafted by hand, mixing island sand and water with concrete from the mainland, so the mechanisation of the process was a welcome time saver. Mum kept a running tally of the number of bricks made and who made them in her diary. Dad never hesitated in asking family and friends who visited them to participate in crafting a brick or two in exchange for his famous CPS Lager, or "swamp water" as many had dubbed it.

TUTOR SISTER AT ROYAL CHILDREN'S HOSPITAL IN BRISBANE

One of Beryl's diary entries that she titled Brick (or Block) Making

A year of momentous events for the Sinclair family

1971

John began his epic fight for K'gari in January 1971 by forming the Fraser Island Defenders Organisation (FIDO). He brought together voluntary conservationists from Maryborough, Hervey Bay, and Bundaberg to oppose sand mining applications by the American Dillingham company and Murphyores.

Murphyores and Queensland Titanium Mines obtained extensive mining leases in the early 1960s without public protest before the voluntary conservation movement became organised. Still, there was widespread public opposition to proposals to extend leases and start mining on the island. Given his emotional connection to the island and our childhood there, John was passionate about protecting the island for future generations.

The organisation's catchphrase of 'FIDO, The watchdog of Fraser Island' captures its ongoing campaigns to ensure the island is a well-managed National Park with controlled tourism and other compatible uses. Its aim is "the wisest use of the natural resources of Fraser Island". I was proud of him for taking a stand and mobilising people to make a real difference.

I intended to further my career and attend the Royal College of Nursing to move into nursing management.

Chris, Charles, Beryl, Jennifer, Margaret, Noel and John at Jen's wedding

In those days, university courses in nursing were not possible to progress, so it was an accumulation of years of experience and completing the proper hands-on training that opened doors to climbing the ranks.

Bridesmaid Margaret with bride Jennifer

Jennifer became an accomplished teacher and has worked as a speech and drama therapist. I was so proud to stand beside her in my handmade gold bridesmaid dress for her wedding day in Easter 1971, which was a huge family affair in Brisbane.

Mum, Jennifer and I were decked out in what I would consider our couture designer ensembles. Mum showed off her fantastic dressmaking skills, making her mother-of-the-bride dress and Jennifer's lovely bridal dress. Then she outdid herself with the stunning silk bouquets that she handmade with the leftover Thai silk from Bangkok. Not to be outdone, I made my bridesmaid outfit.

Little did we know that the photos from that day would be the last of our family of seven. Unfortunately, the official photographer did not take the images with a colour film that day, but the colour coordination was terrific.

After the wedding, and back in my little Brisbane flat at around three in the morning, Chris and I made a pact that the first of us to get married would pay the other $100. My accidental engagement made me realise I didn't want marriage, and it was far from my mind.

It turned out that Chris was to be the next, and it wasn't long before he, too, tied the knot.

Soon after Jen's wedding in April, I slowly moved to Sydney to begin work at the Royal Alexandra Hospital for Children at Camperdown in the Paediatric Intensive Care Unit, where the sickest of children were.

I took a temporary position at the Southport Hospital before moving to Sydney.

This move was an opportunity to become certified in a paediatric intensive care unit, treat medical conditions like leukaemia, and assist with a variety of surgical procedures, such as cardiac surgery.

Royal Alexandra Hospital was a very traditional old hospital that resided in Camperdown for eighty-nine years before moving to Westmead in 1995 to better serve Western Sydney's growing region. This move saw the Royal Alexandra amalgamate with the nearby Westmead Hospital, renamed The Children's Hospital at Westmead.

I lived in the nurses' quarters at the hospital, and while work could be intense, the social life in Sydney was quite interesting. I remember one evening when a phone call invited anyone off duty to a party aboard a Russian submarine docked in Sydney Harbour. A group of the nurses went out there on our night off, and we were plied with straight vodka and partied hard. How much we drank was terrible, but it was so much fun, and we didn't have to drive home!

After arriving in Sydney on September 14, I spent many days off with the family at Locke's home in Petersham. One October Sunday, while sitting around the swimming pool and reading the newspaper, I saw an advertisement with a headline directed at nurses. It was from the Cardiac Surgery Intensive Care Unit at Baylor University Medical Centre in Dallas, and they were looking to fill a one-year contract to staff the new ICU on the night shift.

It sounded intriguing. While I had thought the pinnacle of my career would be to become a matron, I was still too young for such a role, and my mind was open to opportunities. The advertisement announced that interviews would be conducted on Sunday only. I called the number to enquire and was told they had sent a team of recruiters from Dallas, who were interviewing *that* Sunday afternoon. They gave me an address, and I attended the interview a few hours later.

I was most surprised when they announced that I had exceeded my qualifications. My most recent posting at the Royal Alexandra, working in the paediatric ICU, was the icing on the cake, I guess. Plus, I was seven years post-grad and had completed several specialisation certificates. They asked me how soon I could leave for the USA.

I was excited by the prospect of working in a cutting-edge industry within the medical world. At that time, cardiac surgery was still in its infancy since Rene Favaloro performed the first coronary artery bypass graft on May 9, 1967. Baylor University Medical Center was expanding its Cardiac Surgery Unit to keep up with

> ★ ★ ★
>
> MISS Margaret Sinclair former nurse at the Maryborough Base Hospital is spending a few weeks with her parents Mr. and Mrs. C. P. Sinclair, at their home at Eurong, Fraser Island, before leaving Sydney at the end of November to go to the United States.
>
> Margaret has a 12 months' contract in intensive care nursing at the Baylor University Medical Centre in Dallas, Texas.
>
> From there she plans to spend some time in Canada before going to London and the Continent.
>
> During the past six months she has been working at the Royal Alexander Hospital for Children in Sydney.

1971 Oct-Nov newspaper

Talinga Stage 1, 1971

the new procedure, so they recruited Australian nurses to manage the busy night shift.

It was already October, and while my two weeks' notice at the hospital was being completed, Baylor provided me with my H-1B Visa and a one-way Pan American Airways ticket to Dallas. Regulations require H-1B Visa holders to have a bachelor's degree or higher as the minimum educational level. Still, as no such qualification existed in Australia for nurses then, the US Department of Immigration had classified the Australian Nursing Certificates as accepted.

Luckily, I already had a passport, thanks to the cruise I had been on previously. My new grand plan was to complete the contract and travel through Europe for a while before returning to Australia to pick up my goal of attending the Royal College of Nursing. I went to spend a few weeks at Talinga with Mum and Dad.

Breaking the news to my parents was more challenging than I thought. Dad was very quiet and upset. After a moment, he said, "Oh, Marg, you won't return here. You'll meet someone and get married, and we won't see you again."

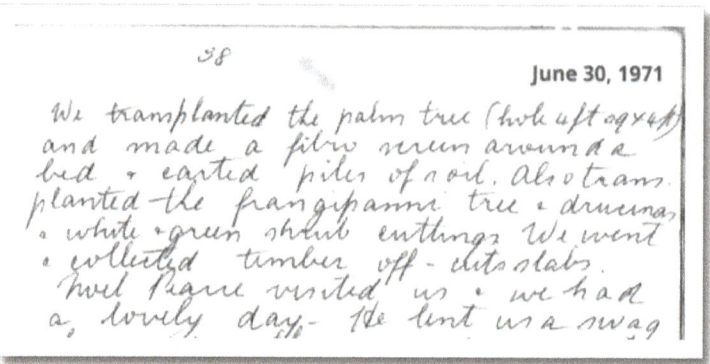

Beryl's diary entry detailing how she planted the palm tree at Talinga

Dad didn't seem convinced by my reassurances that I would return once the contract was complete, but he put it aside so we could enjoy our time together. Talinga felt like home by then, so I found it challenging to imagine how it would be some time before I would have the opportunity to return.

I spent the fortnight saying farewell to friends and family there and getting a final suntan before heading off to winter in the USA. I could see the palm tree Mum had lovingly transplanted on June 30 after it had washed up on shore. She recovered it from the beach after a storm, and to this day, it remains sturdy and unmoving in the place she chose for it.

Noel and Beryl in November, 1971

Word spread that I was going on a vast international adventure, and the Maryborough newspaper ran a small piece about it.

On November 1, my brother Noel, who lived in Bundaberg and worked as a senior executive with the National Mutual Insurance Company, chartered a plane to K'gari and landed on the beach at Eurong for an informal picnic lunch that Mum had prepared on the patio at Talinga.

That day is how I've always remembered him: happy, healthy, fit and vibrant.

I had to fly back to Sydney to pack up my life and head to the US. Because I knew I'd be wearing uniforms most of the time, I managed to fit everything I needed into a single suitcase. I departed on my first International Flight on Pan American Airlines.

After a stopover in Honolulu, I visited Los Angeles, San Francisco, and Las Vegas before arriving in Dallas to start work on December 6, 1971.

I was living in the nurses' quarters at Baylor and going through an orientation program. I didn't know anyone in Dallas except the girls I was working with and a few doctors also working the night shift alongside us.

The nurses' quarters were only for my use until I could find an apartment and settle more permanently into life in the city. Staying in nurses' quarters was fun and made it easier because I did not have the stress of arranging personal accommodation immediately.

I was notified of a telegram for me on Christmas Eve in the mail room. I thought it was probably from Mum wishing me a Merry Christmas, so I didn't rush to retrieve it. When I finally picked it up, I saw it was a Western Union telegram from my brother John.

I was in total shock when I read:

NOEL TRAGICALLY DROWNED CAIRNS, DECEMBER 23rd, *1971.*

Noel was only thirty-four years old, three days before his thirty-fifth birthday on December 26.

He had a lovely wife and five young children under ten, and I felt absolutely at a loss to figure out what had happened. I couldn't reconcile that it had only been a few short weeks since I had seen him and taken a photo of him and Mum at my farewell picnic lunch at Talinga.

I couldn't understand why he was in Cairns, north Queensland, and not at home in Bundaberg. There were so many questions, and I was unfamiliar

Noel with his children, 1971

with the USA's communication systems. I could not call the family on the island because all they had at that time was a two-way radio. I couldn't get in touch with anyone, and there was no way I could find out the details for many months to come.

I didn't have any idea where and when the funeral was to take place. In those days, a trip back to Australia would take thirty-six to forty-eight hours, and I did not have the money to get there so soon after starting a new job in a new country. I felt helpless. Although I had plenty of sympathy and support from my new colleagues, I felt lonely for the first time in my twenty-eight years and didn't know what to do.

Waiting for information over fifty years ago was nothing like it is today. Air Mail took at least five to six days, snail mail took several weeks, and a phone call cost a week's pay! Today, it is hard to imagine the challenges in communications before cell phones, which were not readily available until the 1990s, and the first dial-up internet, America Online, which started soon after that.

A YEAR OF MOMENTOUS EVENTS FOR THE SINCLAIR FAMILY

At a time like that, being with family lessens a massive blow like sudden death, and I couldn't have been further disconnected from mine. With no way to get home, I had to keep working to distract myself from the ache in my heart while I waited for more information. Even with the passage of so much time, I don't think I'll ever get over the shock of losing my brother so young.

When I finally did get all the information, I learned Noel had been swimming in a resort pool with his children when he suffered a cardiac arrest and drowned. John would later tell me he flew with Noel's mother-in-law through Cyclone Anthea to get to Cairns, and the storm had created such severe flooding that the family was isolated in Cairns for four days before they could drive south to Bundaberg for the funeral. I later learned that John and Noel's mother-in-law flew to Cairns to drive the family home.

When I was born, Noel was nearly seven years old, so he was very far ahead in school and education. I am going to post a tribute written to the family by Ian Buckberry in 2002, some thirty-two years after Noel's death.

Ian had so much more information about him than I could ever begin to know:

MY BEST FRIEND NOEL SINCLAIR
Written by Ian Buckberry
October 20, 2002

In a way I had known Noel almost from the moment when I was born for he was born on December 26, 1936, in St Stephens Hospital. Maryborough and I had been born in the same place a few hours earlier on Christmas Day. Our respective parents knew each other but Noel and I attended different primary schools so didn't see much of each other as young children. Our friendship really developed when we reunited and advanced to the Maryborough Intermediate School in our thirteenth year (Year 7).

My earliest memories of Noel are of his love of the bush and camping. He was a member of the local Boy Scout troop and very keen to take me bush to show me the joys of this life. He suggested that we ride our bicycles out to Teddington, a picnic spot around fifteen kilometres from Maryborough. I borrowed the family milk billies, with threats from my parents of terrible retribution should they get damaged. We got out to Teddington after lunch on Saturday and made up a stew and put it on the fire in my billies to simmer through the afternoon.

Then we went down to the creek and constructed a raft of logs lashed together with twine. We toiled all afternoon on this project and as the sun was getting low we conducted a brief ship launching ceremony and pushed the raft into the water. Alas, it barely floated, with only the top of the logs showing and it could not support our weight.

With some sadness we let it drift off downstream. Now, looking forward to a good dinner, we returned to the camp. The fire had died out, but sitting on the embers were two black and twisted billies containing some hardened charcoal. There was to be no dinner and I would have to explain the demise of the milk billies to my parents. Unfazed by these disappointments, Noel set about constructing a *gunya* (temporary shelter) for our evening rest. We laid boughs to lie on and covered the structure with thatching.

After a cup of soup made with vegemite and water and some dry bread, we laid down to rest. But not for long for the evening sky lit up with lightning and thunder rolled louder and louder. Soon the drops of rain turned to steady downpour and water poured through the thatching. We packed our belongings and walked our bikes across the weir to a shelter shed on the opposite bank where we lay down on bare boards but under the shelter of an iron roof Noel remained convinced that his gunya provided great shelter despite the evidence to the contrary.

We often rode our bicycles out to Teddington to swim in the waterhole there. Generally, we were accompanied by Alan Skerritt aka Skerry, the third member of our trio. On arrival, Noel invariably climbed the highest tree and dived into the water. Those below would be shouting up to him that there were rocks and submerged logs in the water but he was unconcerned about such things and dived headfirst into the water with not a care He did this time and time again and never expressed any surprise that he had missed a rock by only inches. He just climbed the tree again and repeated the exercise.

His love of the bush was also satisfied by an annual visit to an uncle who had a dairy farm up near Kingaroy. Noel went there most Christmas holidays and learnt a lot of farming skills, milking cows, horse riding and such like. He would talk about the farm for weeks after his return to school.

We often rode our bikes to Urangan at Hervey Bay, an eighty-kilometre round trip. We generally did this on Saturday or Sunday afternoons and thought nothing of it.

We did four years at school at the Maryborough Intermediate and High School, leaving at the end of our fifteenth year (now Year 10 of school). We were in a class of around thirty boys including some very bright ones, two of whom were Bob White and John Danziger, who both went on to considerable international academic distinction. Bob and John always came first and second in end of term exams but Noel came between third and fifth, never lower. But at the end of Year 10 when teachers and his school mates assumed he would continue to matriculation and go on to university, he left school to assist his father run the family service station. Not once did I hear him complain.

The service station job paid more money than those of his class who took jobs in offices or as apprentices and he had an old 1927 car before long, which was used to ferry all of his mates to our various activities.

Noel loved Fraser Island, which he visited with his parents, Skerry and a few other mates of those times. We planned an Easter at McKenzies on Fraser Island. We went across to the island on Thursday evening and camped on the beach moving up onto a ridge the next morning. Skerry and I had purchased American army plastic tents that Noel scorned as he planned to set up his gunya. Friday was spent setting up camp, digging fireplaces, lashing tables and building Noel's gunya. But a storm came on Friday evening and after about ten points of rain there was a plaintive cry outside my tent and Noel was pleading to come in as it made uncomfortable sleeping for the rest of the weekend but he did not return to the gunya.

Next day a walk across the island to the ocean beach was planned. Noel had a map of the island and a Silva magnetic compass. He professed to know everything about navigation whilst the rest confessed to knowing nothing, so our party set off at a brisk pace behind him. We walked for hours and hours with growing concern from his followers that we might be headed in the wrong direction. But Noel scorned this concern and put all his faith in the map and compass. By about three o'clock, as the sun set lower in the sky it was apparent we were heading westwards and not towards the ocean. There was a revolt and we turned around to return to camp, by this time a seven-hour walking distance. We arrived back by moonlight with everyone exhausted and hungry. Noel took a deal of scolding from his mates over this, but he was unfazed.

Noel had planned the catering but somehow the food ran out by Sunday lunchtime and we were left with flour and peanut paste. We made *puftaloons* out of this—flat cakes baked in the coals and eaten with peanut paste. At the age of seventeen we thought we would starve to death, but the charter boat came for us late on Monday afternoon and took us back to civilisation. It was an expedition none of the participants will ever forget.

In our eighteenth year, Noel and I were called up together for National Service and served in Intake 2 of 1957 in A Company at Wacol. I was in 1 Platoon, and he was in 3 Platoon, so we saw little of each other. Later, we each took our army service seriously and both were commissioned as officers around 1958.

Noel did not drink alcohol but never lectured his mates about its evils. He would drive us to pubs and sit for hours whilst we got sillier and sillier with never a complaint nor any derision if one of us did something stupid or was sick. He was very loyal to his friends and tolerant of their failings and weaknesses.

We attended a tactics course at the Jungle Training Centre at Canungra. On arrival at these courses, Noel would unpack his gear and be settled in whilst I was still trying to unlock my suitcase. He got ready for an exercise in one-tenth the time it took other mortals.

On this course, we had to complete two testing exercises—the Confidence Course and Assault Course. On each he was fearless, running over narrow planks suspended fifty feet above a chasm or charging through barbed wire as if it wasn't there. While observing him in these army exercises (and remembering his shallow water diving exploits as a boy), that he didn't so much as overcome fear but that it wasn't in him. He was truly fearless. Regular army staff at the centre told me that his time over these courses was as fast as anyone had ever achieved

Noel had deep self-assurance and was not humbled should his approach to a task prove to be flawed. I think his mother had brought him up from early childhood to be self-assured and this caused him to make quick decisions without a great deal of analysis of options, to be quite resolute in executing his plans and not to feel any self-doubt if things went wrong in front of colleagues. He did not seem to care what others thought of him as he did what he thought was best at the time without a sideways glance and without later introspection. Sometime after his marriage and the birth of several children, he left the garage and started work as a life insurance salesman with National Mutual. He was most successful and tried to persuade me to follow him. He told me several times: "It is so simple; you just have to do things that everyone else hates doing." Noel had a self-discipline that few others would even begin to understand.

He bought a farm outside Bundaberg and took me out there one afternoon. His energy was overwhelming. He was very busy in his job, played squash, commanded the local army depot, did all the work on the farm and spent a lot of time with his family. I felt exhausted just following him around.

I was living in Adelaide when in December 1971 Skerry phoned to tell me that Noel had died in Cairns. I felt that I had had a leg torn out of my body. I still feel that morning. I don't know all the circumstances, but I imagine that the family drove to Cairns and checked into the motel. Noel would have bounded up to the room, with two suitcases under each arm, whilst everyone else was trying to work out how the air-conditioning system worked Noel would have got completely unpacked changed into swimmers, ran down the stairs and dived into the pool never to surface. How strange is fate—he died in the relative safety of a motel swimming pool yet survived hundreds of carefree dives into shallow rock-filled creeks.

My life was made enormously richer by his friendship. I have never had such a friendship since.

Life in the USA

1971-72

Within a few months of my arrival in Dallas, several other nurses arrived from Australia, and it became clear that our training was highly respected overseas. We had the highest level of direct, hands-on patient care, and in a large, major hospital, we were most likely to have encountered many different diagnoses.

We had to overcome several differences, re-learn some of our Australian teachings, and adapt to the different pronunciations. One significant change was transitioning from the metric system we had become acquainted with in Australia to the old imperial system because the USA had not fully transitioned to metric when most other countries had. Medications were under different brand names, though they were the same generically, and that meant quite an adjustment.

To be allowed to work in our positions, we had to get certification and take the Texas State Board of Nursing Examination. To qualify, we needed to become proficient in the one area not included in our Australian programs and it was essential to getting our boards—psychiatry. So, I took a short course in psychiatry to get me up to speed for the 'boards'.

At the time, psychiatry wasn't part of general nursing in Australia, but it was offered as a separate specialist course for those who wanted to move into it. Even dementia and other mental health conditions were not as prevalent and have increased over time. Back then, psychiatry was different and most serious cases were sent to institutions rather than being cared for in the mainstream medical system.

We had to travel to Austin, Texas, to take our boards, which were held over several days. I never stressed about exams, as my photographic memory helped me to fly through them. It was not uncommon to hear that some nurses had to repeat them before passing. I also received my Critical Care Unit certificate while I was in Dallas.

We also did advanced ICU training and received further qualifications, particularly with the advanced technology used in the units. I learned more about monitoring blood gases to regulate ventilators according to blood work and how to draw arterial blood. At that point, I had received the highest possible qualifications in nursing, which, when added to our exceptional training certificates received in Australia, meant that I could accept very high-level positions in every state in the USA.

American nurses were great to work with, and I soon had many friends, including some Aussie roommates. Living in Dallas was not unlike living in Queensland, and people there were quite taken with our accents and mannerisms.

In the ICU, on the night shift, it was fascinating to see how we all set up our bedside tables in the hallway outside the patient rooms at night. In 1972, smoking was widespread, and nearly everyone smoked. Some of the surgeons would come to visit patients who had undergone coronary bypass or valve surgery that day with a lit cigarette in their hands. Some of the patients had lung surgery, and seeing doctors smoking was so cruel as many of them had been smokers, which more than likely had contributed to their condition.

I was also a smoker then, as it was very trendy! I wasn't until I began to wheeze that I thought it was time to abstain.

The Australian nurses on the night shift usually found accommodation in apartments that were close to the hospital on Gaston Avenue as it was on the bus route to Baylor, so it was safe and easy to get to and from work. After a month or so, I decided to find myself a car so I could move around the city and explore. As I'd had experience with purchasing the Holden when I was living in Sydney, I felt confident as I walked into the used car dealership and started looking around.

I settled on a 1962 Plymouth Fury push button automatic. I had never seen a car like this before, and it was impressive! There was no gear shift. Instead, you pushed the 'Drive' button, and it went forward. Push 'Reverse', and it backed up! It also had a sunroof, which I was quite taken with. I managed to get it for US$100 and drove off in my new car. I had friends with small children eager to wash my car whenever I visited them.

I soon became used to the night shift and adapted to the social events and outings. The Dallas social scene had been quite frustrating, and I became a little disillusioned by the American men, who saw Australian nurses as easy prey. We would head out to a pub called TGI Friday's, which was where the international franchise originated from in Dallas, and the Texas signature drink Harvey Wallbanger cocktails would flow. While we nurses would enjoy each other's company and drink vodka, Galliano, and orange juice drinks, these American guys would do everything they could to run us off to bed. I decided I wanted no part of the dating scene as these American men were just too fast for me.

I decided to get a second shift at the Intensive Care Unit close to Baylor and work part-time from five in the afternoon to 10.30 at night, which I could do several times a

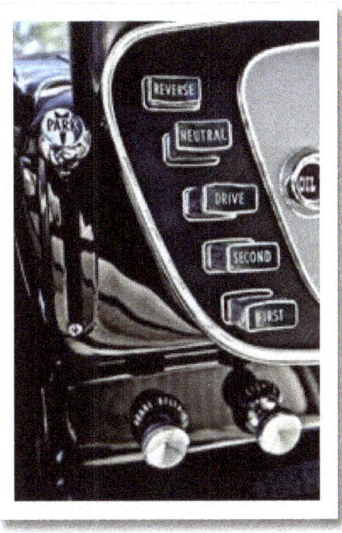

1972 Plymouth Fury

Children of Margaret's friends cleaning her car

week before crossing the road to start the eleven to seven shift at Baylor. After my contract ended, this would be a great opportunity to save enough money to afford a trip to Canada and the UK. With a schedule like that, there was no time for partying, and I enjoyed being busy. At least with a car, I was in control and could go wherever I wanted, whenever I wanted.

By then, I had met some great people through work, and they fulfilled me socially. One of my favourite doctors was Alain Maringo-Rowe, a brilliant haematologist trained at Oxford and Cambridge in the UK. He was recruited to work in our fantastic team when coronary artery bypass surgery was still in its infancy to help with surgical bleeding and clotting problems. Our birthdays were seven years and one day apart. Still, considering the time difference between August 21 in Australia and August 20 in England, we practically shared the same birthday, just seven years apart.

Early in July 1972, while on the night shift at Baylor, I went to the basement vending machines to get myself something to eat while my patient was in the operating room for excessive bleeding. I ran into a new doctor in a scrub suit who was also getting a bite to eat. I had seen him around but hadn't formally met him.

"You're new here?" I asked.

"Yes, I've just arrived from Boston."

His name was Peter Alivizatos, and we had an easy conversation. I discovered he was working with my surgical team and had just joined the group as a Fellow. As he talked about his career, it was clear that he had trained with several highly reputable surgeons, and he was interesting to talk to.

I asked if he had seen much of Dallas, and as he hadn't, I offered to show him around in my fancy car. I picked him up a few days later and showed him the downtown area. In those days, there were limited-height high-rise buildings, and as I pointed them out, I noticed that he was checking out my legs, as I was wearing the latest fashion: 'hot pants'.

We started dating, and Peter and I would see each other professionally in the cardiac surgery unit and in our free time. We would go to a local restaurant for dinner whenever Peter had evenings off. There was an Italian restaurant we liked to frequent, and it was interesting how these big Italian men would arrive in large groups now and then. It turned out that they were the Dallas Mafia. Eating out was lovely, but it reached the point where I was sick of restaurants, so I started cooking for Peter at the apartment instead.

Peter was the perfect gentleman, and we enjoyed each other's company. It was clear from the moment I met him how dedicated he was to his work. He studied a lot in his minimal spare time and was always working on papers to publish. I soon found myself helping him collect data and going through hundreds of charts on the weekends. They kept the cooling on in the doctor's quarters but would switch it off in the offices over the weekends to save money, which made for stifling conditions, but we would be in there anyway, working towards Peter's goal.

The other big mistake I made was letting Peter know I could type. I gradually fell into helping him with his professional communications. He was one hundred per cent a perfectionist, and in those days, we had typewriters, so if you made one mistake, in the absence of correction tape, it meant retyping everything from scratch until it was perfect.

Peter had a secretary, but there were some communications he did not want her to see because he would be looser with his language with some of the recipients, so they fell to me. It became incredibly frustrating when he demanded a letter be typed again for the fifth or sixth time, but he would not send it if it weren't perfect.

Peter was the only person ever to tell me I was lazy. He was never one to mince his words and one evening, he looked at me and said, "You Australian nurses are so smart and such good nurses, but you are party animals, and you don't think. You've got a brain, and don't put it to full use."

It was true; I had always passed my exams with high marks and never needed to study to get where I wanted to go, but I realised he was right. Nobody had ever said anything like that to me before. I felt a strong determination to prove to him that I was intelligent and I could use the brain I had, but I'd never been pushed.

He told me that after he finished his assignment in Dallas, he was returning to Athens, Greece, with Professor Nikos Oeconomos, who needed him to set up an ICU for cardiac surgery at the Hippocration Hospital. The professor also needed a perfusionist, which, in a nutshell, is the medical professional who operates the cardiopulmonary bypass machine during open heart surgery and other procedures in which blood flow is interrupted or impaired. It allows the surgeon to have a 'dry field' because the blood is passed through a machine that oxygenates it and passes it back into the body to continue circulating through the system. Constant monitoring is required to ensure oxygen levels are kept to the patient's required levels.

It's a necessary part of heart surgery, and Peter asked if I might be interested in going to Athens with him to take on the role. I thought that would be an interesting opportunity. Before I knew it, I had agreed to go to Greece with him after his year had passed. This gave me a firm focus on studying to learn the necessary skills.

Peter bought several textbooks and made me sit in a stifling hot office on weekends and study. I don't think I could have achieved half of what I'd go on to accomplish professionally without Peter continuously challenging me to be better.

Before long, Peter had me training with the Baylor technicians. As I already had two jobs, I would go to the operating room as soon as I finished my night shift at seven and stay for the first case every morning. Then, I would go home to sleep for a few hours before working my usual shifts. I had only a few months to become proficient at this technology before taking on the role in Athens.

I taught myself to read and write the fantastic Greek language using textbooks. However, Peter refused to speak to me in Greek, but I persisted. Learning how to put my skills into practice through conversation had to wait until I got there!

∼

Before our international move, Peter and I went to Houston, Texas, to spend time working with world-renowned American cardiac surgeons and doctors, Denton Cooley and Michael DeBakey.

Dr. Cooley was an American cardiothoracic surgeon famous for performing the first implantation of a total artificial heart. Cooley was also the founder and surgeon-in-chief of The Texas Heart Institute, chief of cardiovascular surgery at clinical partner Baylor St. Luke's Medical Center, consultant in cardiovascular surgery at Texas Children's Hospital and a clinical professor of surgery at the University of Texas Health Science Center at Houston.

Dr. DeBakey was a cardiovascular surgeon, scientist and medical educator who became Chairman of the Department of Surgery, President, and Chancellor of Baylor College of Medicine at the Texas Medical Center in Houston, Texas.

Houston was where most of the groundbreaking heart surgery work was being done in the US at the time, and it looked close enough to Dallas on the map. Peter and I had never been on a road trip like this before. We were unprepared, setting off without knowing when to reach the destination. To make matters worse, we ended up with a flat tyre on the way and fixing that ate into precious time. It took us six hours to get there, and Peter was late for his meeting with Dr. Cooley. Unfortunately, Dr. DeBakey was operating from another hospital then, but I met him when he visited Greece while I was working there.

By that stage, I had learned how to run the heart-lung machine, and this was a priceless opportunity for us to see the best in the business in action. I spent time with the perfusionist while Peter was working with Dr. Cooley.

Dr. Cooley and his team performed twenty cardiac surgeries in six operating rooms daily. Each room had its own team, and Dr. Cooley would go from one room to the next and perform the actual procedure while the teams had the patients on the bypass pump ready for him and closed the chest after he worked his magic. It was something to behold, and I am sure I will never see anything like that again—a performance by a true master!

We spent an entire week there, and it was phenomenal to see what was possible when you had a well-coordinated team and processes in place. Every member of the team was meticulous in their work. In those days, if you had coronary artery stenosis—which affects blood flow to the heart—the surgical procedure was very invasive as you had to remove the blocked artery and replace it with a vein from the patient's arm or leg. Now, most blockages can diagnosed and treated by a cardiologist via X-ray, making the surgical coronary bypass open heart procedure rarely necessary.

Cyclone Daisy strikes Talinga

1972

I was so busy that year that I had few opportunities to catch up with my family in Australia. Since comparing Mum's diary for that period, I understand how busy they had been at Talinga.

Because so much had happened in December 1971, my parents were given very little notice, and they finally sold the family home on Tooley Street, Maryborough.

168 Tooley Street, 1970

All it meant was that they no longer had the financial tie to the town and could move ahead with plans for extensions for Talinga. But before they could get around to that, the island was hit by several cyclones, the worst of which was Cyclone Daisy, when the eye hit Eurong with its full force.

Mum's diary held details of the harrowing events:

Monday, January 14, 1972

Daisy has come and gone, so I will repeat her rampage in detail. She was a vicious little minx. On Thursday evening, I slept in the lower back bunk after taping windows and placing sewing baskets, wool, and other items on beds under plastic coverings. The wind was wild, but I slept with the back door ajar. I only woke three times, but I kept the radio going all night just in case.

Friday came wild, and it soon seemed that we would not miss it. I did what I could and waited. I was pleased to see Charlie with a forestry vehicle again, along with Doug and Ken. It was getting wild by then, but we replaced the cushion mattress on the seat and had lunch, after which the boys inspected all the neighbours to check how things were going and if they were prepared. By 1.45 pm, when the boys left, they thought the wind was 95 miles per hour. The vehicle was shaking as though ready to take off. They had a nightmare trip back, details of which we know little except for a snippet of news on the radio.

By 2.30 pm, the blasts were much more severe. I had a bucket of food supplies ready, a thermos, and a packed port near the back door, and I settled down calmly to crochet while Charlie pottered around, mopping up a bit of water seeping in.

Suddenly, I saw our taped windows and the whole front wall bulging inward and shaking. Then Charlie yelled for help as we saw the side door (S end) bulge inward, and water streamed in.

After mopping several buckets of water, we gave up and faced significant trouble with the door. So, I found a 3'x 2' pine board tabletop (fortunately handy) and took it from the hut to keep march

> flies out of the washing tubs. The gusts became so intense that our arms, wrists, and shoulders became sore.
>
> We heard many mysterious bangs but were too busy to see much, except our outer branches of the pandanus were gone and draped with the old, distorted banana lounge—blown from under the house.
>
> Then the fibro from the door (nailed on the outside for protection) and a pane of glass went, and we were just flat out and exhausted. Charlie realised he was getting tired at 5.30 after dealing with strong gusts, bumps, and bursts of noise. It eased, but we still held the door in case of another gust.

Neighbours came to help hold up the door so my parents could survey the damage. While the garden was a mess and unsecured furniture had been blown around and destroyed, Talinga was still upright.

John wrote about this in his book *Fighting for Fraser Island*:[5]

> This house, originally little more than a two-roomed weekender, had provision for an extension on the southern wall with a boarded-up door. This wall was not constructed to withstand a tempest like Daisy.
>
> Charlie and Beryl quickly realised that as the storm blasted open the boarded-up door, which was beginning to give, the house could explode from the inside out.
>
> They piled all available furniture against the door while the storm howled around them, but the weak spot continued to give. Charlie braced himself against the barricade and remained there for twelve hours, straining against the immense force outside and adjusting to the shifting pressure points.
>
> Eventually, the eye of the storm passed right over them, and the wind abated. The house remained unchanged, but Charlie experienced such extreme stress that he was incapacitated for weeks, barely able to use a knife and fork or lift a glass of his prized homemade brew to his lips.

If it hadn't been for their presence, the cyclone would have blown in the door, which would have meant losing its roof. Dad had piled up every bit of furniture and used his entire body force to prevent it from giving way. He suffered and was really in pain for some time afterwards, but he was happy he was there to save the house.

John had been able to charter a plane over the island with a TV news crew to survey the damage and got a message to our parents by dropping a brick with a note taped and tied to it from the plane.

Chris married Deanne Laidlaw on May 5, 1973, shortly before being posted to Townsville in July. Unfortunately, it was another one of many family weddings that I could not attend, as I was completing my training in preparation for our move to Greece in the coming months

They have three children, Karen, Julie, and David, and seven grandchildren.

Chris and Deanne with Beryl and Charles on their wedding day

Working in Athens

1973

I arrived in Athens alone a few weeks before Peter, who had to spend some time in Boston at a conference. On my arrival, I was met by a concierge from Professor Economos' wife's hotel. She owned several hotels across the city and I was to stay at the closest one to the Hippocration Hospital until I could find more permanent accommodation.

The hotel was very nice, but being in the business district of Athens, directly across the road from the Polytechnic College, it was quite a hive of activity due to the growing unrest with student protests.[6] The Polytechnic was regarded as a symbol of resistance against the Greek military dictatorship (junta) that year and minor protests and strikes started in February. It all came to a head at the Polytechnic on November 14 when a Greek army tank crashed through the institution's gates. The events that followed led to the death of dozens of people and the injury of more than 2,000 before the junta was overthrown in early 1974.

My assignment with the professor was from September 1, 1973, until the end of June 1974. On my arrival, the professor instructed me to request the concierges' services if there was anything I needed. I felt somewhat stifled without transportation, as I would have done in any other place I lived, so I decided to get myself a car.

With my basic Greek and the concierge's broken English, he took me to a used car dealership that specialised in used imports with international number plates. I had learned that if I purchased a car with Greek plates, I would have to pay hefty taxes. While the car was in Greece, I could own a vehicle with foreign license plates and avoid Greek taxes.

Upon arriving at the dealership, I saw a beautiful Alfa Romeo Giulietta Super with Italian license plates. It was a reasonably late model and cost about US$100, almost all my money. Unfortunately, I had not checked the petrol price in Greece. I was used to filling up in the US for $1.50 per gallon and was shocked when I took my Giulietta to the gas station for the first time and found it was going to cost ten times as much.

This meant the Alfa was parked outside our apartment for two weeks a month, as I only had enough salary to drive the car for the remainder of the month. Once the tank ran out, I would take the bus to the hospital until my next pay check arrived.

Peter's family was warm and welcoming, and they fully accepted me. I was amazed at how eager they were to help me in any way they could. In contrast to my lack of worldly knowledge and having grown up in the 'new world,' they were traditionally Greek and had little exposure to neophytes.

Peter was their pride and joy and their only child. He had a cousin, also called Peter Alivizatos. His cousin was also an only child, not much younger, and the two men were more like brothers.

I first met his great family when they were quite elderly. Peter's mother, Tasia, was blind to glaucoma, but somehow, she would use her gentle touch and feel. I don't know how, but she understood me very well. His father, Alekos, had been a journalist and had some ability to understand

Margaret's Alfa Romeo Giulietta Super was her pride and joy in Athens

my broken Greek. He didn't hesitate to communicate with me in English as much as possible. There was such a contrast of nationality, heritage, culture, education, environment and language, being just a few.

Peter was surrounded by his three maiden aunts (which means unmarried), who were at his beck and call. Aunt Fofo was his mother's sister, while Kate and Maria were his father's sisters.

Before my arrival, my Greek had been limited to reading and writing the foreign alphabet from textbooks. I had no verbal experience, so Aunt Katy, Peter's 86-year-old maiden aunt, took it upon herself to give me Greek lessons. That often ended in shrieks of laughter bringing down the whole house when I would put the emphasis on the wrong syllable and end up with a pronunciation of a simple word like 'soft' being translated into the English equivalent of 'masturbator'. That is something that I never lived down!

Peter with his parents on the right and Aunt Kate, 1974

Fortunately, I found that most educated people had studied English in school, so it was easier for me to learn the Greek language at a slower pace.

Peter's Uncle Gerasimos Alivizatos was an internationally recognised hygiene authority and creator of the rabies vaccine. He was heavily involved in the World Health Organization when it was first formed. He was highly respected, and I was impressed by his acceptance of me. My most exciting memory of Uncle Gerasimos was when he purchased tickets to Vagner's Flying Dutchman opera at the opera house. He dressed in his evening attire and proudly wore me on his arm. That was one of the most beautiful experiences of my life and the very first opera I had experienced, made even more impressive by the ancient Greek Opera House.

With my car and a strong connection to Peter's family, my next challenge was finding accommodation near the hospital where we would work. I settled in Psychiko, one of the wealthiest suburbs of Athens, which has very high land values and many embassies.

Fortunately, an Italian couple owned a charming, small, furnished apartment in a great position available for rent. I kept Peter informed of my progress through letters, which we wrote to each other just about every day. He was quite shocked that I had set myself up comfortably so quickly before I was due to start work.

As the professor's assistant, I was paid US$300 per month, more than the doctors who worked with him. My responsibilities were to set up the ICU for post-operative cardiac care, be the professor's perfusionist in the operating room, and train the nursing personnel to operate the ventilators, read blood gases, and interpret electrocardiograms (ECGs). I learned most of these skills during my ICU training in Dallas.

I was scheduled to assist the professor in surgery for the first time before Peter arrived in Greece, so I mentally prepared before going to the hospital that day. I knew what I had to do, and I'd seen the best in the world perform the surgery; this was my time to put it all into action.

Before that morning, I had met the team, including the anaesthesiologist, but this would be our first time in an operating room together. I noticed when I started to perform my blood bypass procedures with the blood oxygenator machine that the blood was unusually thick. Usually, the anaesthesiologist administers a drug called heparin, which prevents the blood from naturally clotting so it can flow unobstructed through the machine. I didn't know the anaesthesiologist well enough to feel it was appropriate to question whether they had carried out all the steps before it was my turn to step in. I assumed they were a professional who knew what they were doing. That was a frightening experience for me and meant many changes had to be made before we were ready for the next case.

I was so happy to see Peter when I picked him up at the airport. We had an interesting conversation that started with, "Do you happen to know somebody called Jeff from Perth? He seems to know you very, very well..."

Oh my gosh! I knew who he was talking about instantly. *How on earth would Peter meet Jeff?*

I met Jeff while I was completing my midwifery accreditation in Perth. We got to know each other quite well as the midwives would teach the medical students, and we started dating, although it never became serious. To this day, I don't know the exact details of how they met in Boston, but I imagine Peter hearing Jeff's Australian accent, striking up a conversation and then realising he was from Perth. Once he mentioned that my parents lived on Fraser Island, it would have been quite an awkward exchange... Peter found it hilarious.

As the professor's surgical assistant, Peter slotted seamlessly into the Hippocration Hospital team. As our ICU was brand new, Peter had a specific idea of how he wanted it to run. Whenever we had a cardiac bypass procedure, I was required to be in the operating room until the patient was transferred to recovery, and Peter would not leave the hospital unless I stayed with the patient. Sometimes, this meant that at least one of us was on call for twenty-four hours until the patient was fully stabilised.

This would give patients immediate medical attention if there were any complications, and this practice was one of the many things that cemented Peter's reputation for having survival rates that matched the best in the world. He was the ultimate perfectionist, and that served him tremendously well in his career.

In my role, I was responsible for finding nursing staff for the ICU. Through that recruitment process, I met a lovely, highly qualified British nurse named Clair Cheetham from the UK, who was married to a British

Margaret with Clair Cheetham and her husband and another friend in Athens

Peter and Margaret with the Greek friendship circle, 1973

diplomat. Clair and I bonded instantly, and she became one of my very special lifelong friends.

Working with Clair and socialising with her British Embassy friends on our days off made for some of my most memorable experiences in Athens.

Clair was an excellent nurse and, in 2025, is still working in Houston, specialising in caring for high-risk obstetric patients. She has become invaluable and is one of her field's most highly respected nurse practitioners in Houston, Texas. To this day, I can still pick up the phone and talk for hours with her, no matter where we live. Friends like this have made my life so complete.

As Peter had lived in Greece for most of his life before becoming a doctor, there was no shortage of people from his social circle for me to meet. I was readily introduced to them and developed some great friendships.

Several of Peter's friends had Anglo partners who could speak English. Without them, his friends would often get into lengthy and heated political conversations in Greek, which were too difficult for me to interpret, so I became very good at tuning out and nodding when I thought it appropriate.

Life was never dull for me, although these social get-togethers often went into the wee hours of the morning. In those days, the Greeks used to work in the mornings until noon, then have a three-hour lunch with siesta before returning at around four and working a few more hours before a late evening meal.

Our little furnished apartment at Psychiko was fun, and I enjoyed polishing my entertaining skills.

The professor asked me if I would take care of an excellent friend of his. My patient, Mr Kambanis, was a Greek Aristocrat who had been the best man at King Constantine II's wedding to Queen Anne-Marie on September 18, 1964, just six months after Constantine had been crowned King.[7]

When I met Mr Kambanis in late 1973, he was in feeble health with bronchiectasis, a condition in which lungs remain stiff and are permanently damaged. As I had been used to caring for hospital patients and was familiar with bronchial lavage, I agreed to work privately for him. He and his wife were wonderful people and lived close to Peter's parents.

I visited him three times a week, and his wife decided I should get some Greek cooking lessons from her chef. Once a week, her maid would give me a lesson on whatever was on the menu, and I learned how to make her recipes the traditional Greek way. Peter was very impressed that I learned how to prepare *melitzanosalata*, an eggplant salad, authentically with a wooden spoon and a wooden board.

I am proud to say that my patient responded very well to my therapy, a regime of weekly physiotherapy on his lungs and suctioning out excess mucous to allow him to breathe more easily. Both the professor and I believe this regime extended his life significantly.

Mr Kambanis was a joy to be around, and I think he enjoyed having his young nurse care for him! His wife was warm and beautiful and after Mr

Margaret with Mr Kambanis

Margaret was gifted a beautiful watercolour painting of the Arch of Hadrian by Mr Kambanis' wife

Kambanis died, she called me to say that her husband wished to give me a painting in appreciation for his care.

With that, she pointed to a pair of magnificent paintings by a famous turn-of-the-century Greek watercolourist. They were of the Arch of Hadrian, also known as Hadrian's Gate, which was built in 132 AD.

It remains one of my most treasured possessions.

My Godmother, Mary Hecker, and Marjorie Alexander, two of Mum's very close friends, called in to check on me while we were in Athens on a long cruise and met Peter for the first time.

On their return to Australia, they reported back to my parents that everything was great and gave their seal of approval that I was in good and safe hands.

Mary Hecker with Peter in Athens

War in Cypress and a hasty escape to Australia

1974

The Turkish invasion of Cyprus began on July 20, 1974, just a few weeks after my contract at the Hippocration Hospital was interrupted for the summer.[8] The conflict was the Turkish military response to a coup, which the Cypriot National Guard had staged against President Makarios III with the intention of annexing the island to Greece. The invasion came after more than a decade of sporadic inter-communal violence between the islands Greek Cypriots and Turkish Cypriots.

I was in Syntagma Square getting the bus back to my apartment and had a machine gun stuck in my ribs by a passing soldier. It was clear that this was the beginning of the official coup.

Soon, tanks were in the streets, and the airports were closed in anticipation of military action. To keep me safe, Peter suggested it would be the perfect time for me to go back to visit my family in Australia. He, on the other hand, planned to stay and fight for his country. He knew what he was doing, and he was always passionate about national affairs and his duty to his country, so I had no trouble accepting his wishes.

The coup was in effect so we hatched a spontaneous plan for me to drive to Patras, where I could still leave the country by boarding a ferry to Brindisi in Italy. I would find assistance to help me sell the car at my landlord's home, who lived in Rome. After selling the car, I planned to board a plane from Rome to Brisbane.

It was a simple plan, and it seemed like everything would easily fall into place. Peter dusted off his uniform, and I drove him in. We said goodbye, and I said I'd wait to see him walk through the gates before I left. He approached the guard station and spoke with the officer on duty. I didn't have to wait long before Peter returned to the car, clutching his military knapsack containing his uniform in one hand, with his metaphorical tail between his legs.

"They wouldn't take me," he said. "They said I was too old." I felt sorry for him, but it became something we were able to laugh about quickly afterwards. So, Peter drove to Patras with me and caught the train back to Athens while I purchased a ticket to Brindisi. Even if he had been able to come with me, the reality was that we couldn't afford it. I was surprised we'd had enough for my ferry ticket and plane fare because Peter was not paid very well for his work, and we did not have much money.

I boarded the ferry to Brindisi with nothing more than my passport, a plane ticket from Rome to Brisbane, a small amount of cash and car papers. I had no idea exactly how far Brindisi was from Rome. I had the address and a sense of optimism that there would not be a problem.

It all went well until I drove the car to the ferry terminal exit. Because I had foreign licence plates, the terminal worker demanded to see my car papers and, upon inspection, told me I was not allowed to leave the terminal until I purchased insurance for the vehicle—even though I would only have it for another twenty-four hours. I pleaded with him, but he would not relent. No payment, no exit.

The 'insurance' would cost most of the cash I had with me, but I handed the money over with no choice, which was probably pocketed. After driving for a few hours on the *Autostrada*, I realised I would soon need petrol. Not familiar with the road systems in Italy, I found it quite challenging to find a gas station. In the US, you could usually see them from the highways, but I hadn't seen one for hours and realised I had to exit the *Autostrada* and drive into the suburbs to find a gas station.

Another thing I did not realise at the time was that it was a long weekend in Italy, so everything was closing earlier than usual. I finally found a station that was about to close. I pulled in but didn't have the language to ask for what I wanted. That was only a minor problem once I realised I didn't have Italian currency.

This was a major problem because the attendant had already filled up my tank. There were no credit cards in 1974, and the international currency was traveller's checks, which I had not been able to get in Greece because it was a weekend and I had departed so hastily.

The attendant put his hand through the window, and I handed over some Greek drachma. He returned with the change, which he passed to me through the driver's window. He dropped the change and immediately reached down. I thought it would be to help me locate the coins, but instead, he suddenly started groping me. I panicked but had the tenacity to roll the window up on his arm quickly.

Realising he was stuck, he started yelling at me. I lowered the car just enough for him to pull his arm free, and I took off. I was petrified. *What am I doing?* I had no idea where I was going and trusted that if I stayed on the *Autostrada*, I would eventually get to Rome.

Peter had warned me many times not to pick up hitchhikers, but as I re-entered the *Autostrada*, I saw a friendly-looking couple I had seen on the ferry. When I stopped to ask if they were okay, I discovered they wanted to go to Rome, so I picked them up. Ultimately, it was a great decision, as having the company made me less afraid. The couple were from South Africa, and we got to know each other as the miles passed. We finally got to Rome after travelling all night with a few coffee stops, many of which I would have been too scared to do as a single female in the middle of the night. I was unprepared and didn't even have as much as a single bottle of water to sustain me for the trip, so these pitstops were vital.

After dropping them off in Rome, I had to find my way to my landlord's villa without a GPS, which was still a few decades away from development. I didn't even have a local paper map to use, so I stopped to ask people now and then.

When I pulled up at this beautiful villa, I was greeted by a scared-looking maid who did not speak or read English or Greek. Through hand gestures, I discovered they were away for the long weekend and wouldn't return until the next day. I found a pensione to stay overnight and returned later the next day to find them at home.

When the landlord saw my car papers, he advised me that I owned a stolen car that couldn't be sold in Italy. He explained that an international ring stole vehicles in Italy and dropped them off at dealers in Athens for foreigners to purchase without paying Greek taxes. While I owned the car in Greece, there was no problem, but that probably explains why I could buy a beautiful Alfa Romeo at such a great price!

I drove to the airport with very little cash left but at least a plane ticket to Australia. I decided it was best to abandon the car, keys, and everything else in the parking garage, as I did not want to be caught in possession of a stolen vehicle. I saw my car again many years later on the big screen while watching one of the new James Bond releases. I swear my Giulietta—same colour and everything—was used in a car chase scene that happened to be set in Italy. I could never prove it, though, and I still take every opportunity to search the old James Bond movies in the hope of seeing my lovely car again.

It was unnerving walking through the airport in Rome past security guards with machine guns. I felt such great relief when I finally boarded my plane, but I was quickly overcome by the overwhelming smell of garlic that enveloped the cabin. There was no genetically modified garlic back then, and the Italians ate so much garlic with their meals that the smell would come out of people's pores. It wafted over me as people reached to put their luggage in the overhead compartments.

During a sweltering three-hour stopover in Delhi, I had very little change left in my purse, but I managed to call my sister, Jen, to ask that she meet her destitute sister at the airport. I finally made it to Brisbane and could breathe a massive sigh of relief. I found out Jennifer had won $100,000 in the lottery, so they were more than happy for me to stay a while to get back on my feet.

It was an excellent lesson for a highly confident, single, thirty-one-year-old who had managed to solve most problems without help: Sometimes, you need a second opinion when dealing with such huge issues. I just hadn't ever thought that some problems might need help. Indeed, had I been able to plan a trip like this properly, I would have had all sorts of help available, but who could imagine that a war would close airports and getting to Australia at short notice would have been such an issue? Looking back now, it could have been a lot worse!

Back home at Talinga

1974

Arriving in Australia after all these tremendous unplanned discoveries made me somewhat cynical about materialism. After living in an ancient country like Greece, where people made every penny count, it was hard to accept that most people have enough to indulge in whatever they wanted in modern wealthy countries like the USA and Australia.

After spending a few days with Jenny and Ray at their new home in MacGregor, I was off for another few days with Chris and to meet his wife

Charles fishing with Pundi at Eurong, 1974

Dee for the first time since their marriage the previous year. Their baby daughter, Karen, was just a few months old when I met them all in Canungra.

From there, I spent time at Talinga with Mum and Dad and their two dogs, Pundi and Cassius, a new labrador pup.

Dad was not as fit and energetic as when I last saw him in 1971, and he had slowed down a lot. Losing his eldest son was a significant blow for him. He was still the amazing man he had always been, without the oomph.

In 1974, he was ordered back into the field, felling trees. At sixty and with his arthritic knees, the physical toll was too much for him to manage, but he stuck it out for weeks because he and Mum needed an income.

Unfortunately, a scrub tick bored into his back while he was working, and he ended up very sick with scrub typhus, which led to an angina diagnosis. While the doctor cleared him for work, his employer refused to allow him to return, forcing him to retire. John seemed to think this had something to do with the fact that he had been making great headway with bringing logging companies to account for their activities on the island, and our father was a scapegoat for their frustrations.

Dad's two dogs kept him busy since he no longer had the responsibilities of his work at the forestry, but he was always willing to help anyone in need. He worked on landscaping Talinga, helped Mum with her constant projects, and socialising.

By then, John was also bringing his FIDO friends and colleagues home to visit them, so there was no shortage of neighbourly contact and always the Happy Hour drinks with his homebrew, which had its own identity— CPS Lager. He and his good friend Muir Daniels had distinctive brews competing for perfection. Dad never failed to toast all the "poor" people who could not be there to share the Island life with us.

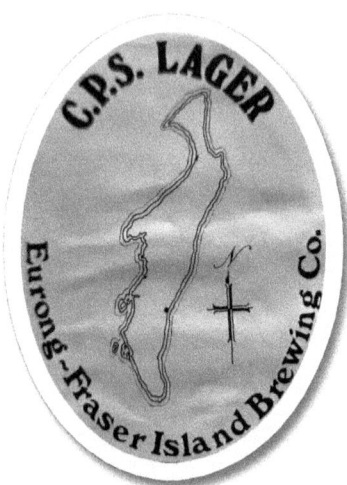

The label of Charles' famed CPS Lager

He did plenty of little things to keep himself busy, like making coloured sand bottles by layering the different colours of sand collected from Cathedral Rocks.

Those days were beautiful. There was no electricity, phones, or television, and there were rarely any interruptions. After dinner, we would use a hurricane or gas lamp to play Cribbage or Scrabble until bedtime.

Charles with Casius and Pundi at Eurong

Although we had a generator for power, they were much smaller then and very noisy, and besides, lamp lights created a much nicer ambience.

The sunrises over the ocean were always spectacular, and it was such a pleasure to be woken up by the sun and go for a long beach walk or fish before breakfast.

Dad had purchased a Kipper Box, so we spent time together fishing early in the morning until it was smoking, ready for the day's catch.

Those days, Pundi would sit for hours watching the brumbies on the beach. The Fraser Island Brumby is a distinct breed created through the interbreeding of the Clydesdale horses brought to the island in the 1800s to help with the logging industry and the Arab horses trained on the island by the Australian Army in the late 1900s. The Arab horses were used in the Boar War and eventually WWI.[9]

As some escaped or were released once their duties were fulfilled, they could interbreed and create a unique horse.

Pundi also took on the responsibility of keeping a close watch for a dingo or two, as they used to taunt Cassius. The dingos, which have white markings on their feet, tips of their tails, and chests, are not actually wild dogs. They are, in fact, their own species, Canis *dingo*.[10]

Dingoes are highly flexible, with double-jointed limbs and necks that can turn 180 degrees in any direction, a feat impossible for dogs. In addition to these unique characteristics, dingoes are excellent runners, jumpers and climbers. They have been tracked at sixty kilometres an hour and travelling forty kilometres in one day. They can bound two metres high and successfully climb trees.

In those days, there were no dingo fences around Eurong village, and the dingo howls at night were sometimes quite haunting. We never feared them because they always found their food, so they kept their distance. I was more fearful of the cane toads because they were slimy and gross when I stood on one at night.

I don't remember what dates I was with Mum and Dad when I came home for those few weeks, but I found my name in the visitor's book Mum always kept, with my signature on September 4, 1974.

The move from Greece to the USA

1975

Following my return to Athens, it was time for Peter and I to make important career decisions. My contract with the professor in Athens concluded during the summer break, when everyone in Greece stopped working and went off for holidays, virtually shutting up shop for a few weeks. It was a time when it got unbearably hot, and with no air-conditioning and hot breezes, this hiatus was easy to understand. I continued to work with my private patient and visited his summer home in the hills, where the temperature was several degrees cooler.

Peter was becoming very pessimistic about his future in Greece. While the professor had been nothing but good to me, he seemed more interested in having Peter as his assistant in perpetuity. That was unacceptable to Peter because being in that role would not allow him to advance his surgical interests. He was much more ambitious and growing tired of feeling stuck in a place where he could no longer move forward.

Peter was pleased with the cardiac surgery skills he had acquired in the USA, and I knew he would never be happy being a general surgeon. We had a few agonising months in which I could only see him happy if he could do the necessary training to complete the 'boards' to qualify in the USA fully.

FORMER CITY NURSE IS EMPLOYED IN ATHENS

A former Maryborough girl, Margaret Sinclair, returned home recently from Greece where she operated the heart-lung machine at the University of Athens Medical School.

Margaret, a nursing sister, is the daughter of Mr. and Mrs. Charlie Sinclair, formerly of Maryborough and now living on Fraser Island.

She is a very much travelled young woman, having worked in hospitals throughout Australia, in America and in Greece.

She did her first two years of nursing in Maryborough after leaving Maryborough High School, and completed her training at Princess Alexandra Hospital in Brisbane.

Found her niche

Since then she has done midwifery and pediatrics in Sydney and Perth. She left for Dallas, Texas, in 1971, and it was there she found her niche in the medical profession.

She was working in a cardio-thoracic intensive care unit when she was given the opportunity to study the heart-lung machine with a well-known U.S. heart surgeon.

She mastered the technique to the extent that she was able to work with the famous heart transplant surgeon, Dr. Cooley, when he was carrying out research work on a nuclear pacemaker. She did not assist at any actual heart transplants with Dr. Cooley.

Margaret said she felt much more had to be learnt about heart transplant and associated problems before they would again be performed on the scale of four or five years ago.

Most impressed

Margaret was most impressed by the extremely high standard of medicine in the United States and by the high level of training given to para medical staff.

She said she had had to pass the American Registration Board examinations before she could work in U.S. hospitals as a sister.

While at Dallas Margaret worked with a visiting Greek medical man, Professor Oeconomos, from the University of Athens' Medical School and it was on his invitation that she took up her appointment in Greece just over a year ago.

On account of her specialist qualification on the heart-lung machine, she is accorded what amounts to doctor status and she and Dr. Alivizatos, the professor's assistant, established the first intensive care unit at the Hippocration Hospital, which is the University Hospital.

She loves her work and is involved in all major surgery there. After all big operations she is with the patient for at least the first 24 hours — sometimes 24 hours straight.

Recovery miracles

She said she has seen dedication on the part of Dr. Alivizatos bring about 20th century "miracles" of recovery.

She said great advances were being made in medicine in Greece, and patients who would have had no chance a few short years ago now made the grade. There was a more sophisticated knowledge of respirators and blood gases, electro cardiographs, monitoring and defibrillation.

She feels she will probably stay in Greece another year. She said prices were very high, but she loved the people, who were exceptionally friendly and extremely generous.

She said she could talk some Greek, but at work most of the doctors spoke English. She used Greek when talking to nurses or when out shopping.

Junta in power

She said she was in Athens when the military junta was in office but had not noticed much restriction on freedom until the new Government came to power after the Cyprus trouble and the people began to enjoy real freedom again.

She said one of the nicest things that had happened to her since her arrival in Greece was a visit from her godmother, Mrs. Sam Hecker, of Maryborough.

Margaret left Maryborough on Sunday on the first leg of her return journey to Greece.

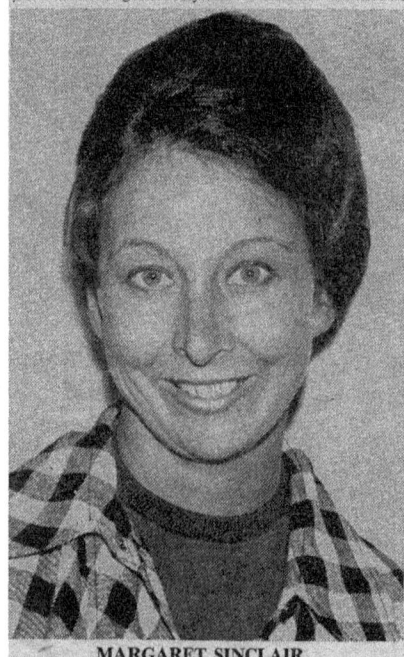

MARGARET SINCLAIR

Newspaper article about Margaret's Greece experience

From there, he could move forward to a much more fulfilling career. He had worked with some of the best cardiac surgeons in the world in Boston and Dallas when cardiac surgery was still in its infancy. With so much innovation happening in that field, I knew that was precisely where Peter needed to be in order to be satisfied with his career.

Now, it was time for me to make my own decisions. I did not feel that there was a future for me in Greece without Peter, and I did not want to return to the USA and go through all the immigration issues to work anywhere other than Dallas. When we evaluated the possible scenarios, we eventually decided that marriage might be the best solution for both of us and got engaged. There was no romantic gesture or surprise proposal; it was all very perfunctory.

Peter and I were an improbable couple; we were so different in many ways. He was from a highly cultural background and a true academic, while I decided to leave school at sixteen. He was an only child, while I was one of five siblings. He was from an ancient society with huge traditions, while I was from "the new world". He was from the northern hemisphere, and I was from "down under". While Peter was completely fluent in English and ancient Greek, I spoke English and very little Greek.

The only things we had in common were our professions and a mutual admiration and respect for each other.

"You know Peter, I don't think that my parents are going to really appreciate me running all over the world with you and going back to the States again unless there's a different arrangement." Peter thought about it and agreed. He wrote to my parents to inform them that we intended to get married, to their delight, even though they had never met him. I also had to let them know that we were going to move back to the US.

From then, my parents began to communicate to Peter's parents through letters back and forth. I'm not sure how this was all interpreted, as Mum tended to express herself very well in her native dialect and although Peter's father was great with words, his understanding of written English was not as developed as his spoken word. Nevertheless, they managed, and I thought it was great that they developed that relationship even though they had not met one another.

Peter's parents were overjoyed and his Aunt Fofo bought us both rings. In Greece, it is customary to both wear rings from the moment of engagement and it automatically becomes your wedding ring once you are married, so you only must buy one.

Peter chose to move forward with his ambition to be qualified in cardiac surgery and be free to work in any country at the same level as locally trained citizens. His first step to be able to achieve this was to complete another two years of surgery residency in the USA.

After that decision, it seemed that my best option was to return to Dallas, where I could again work as a perfusionist at Baylor, and in the Cardiac Surgery ICU for a few months until our immigration status was cleared and then join Peter in Boston. I couldn't go directly to Boston with my new fiancé because Baylor had sponsored my work visa and therefore it was the only place I could legally work. Luckily, they wanted me back anyhow and it was great to go back to a place I already knew before moving to Boston!

Peter and I flew back to the USA together and after Peter disembarked in Boston, I continued on to Dallas. We became great correspondents, once again writing to each other most days. Peter was a wonderful communicator and could capture a lot in his letters, so it made me feel like we were still close even though we were miles apart.

I felt very much at home in Dallas, as I had quite a few friends, having lived there for over two years from 1971 to 1973. Time passed quickly as I counted down the six months it would take for Peter to apply for permanent residency. This was vital for our plan because once he was approved, our marriage would give me the same privileges and I would then be free to work anywhere in the US.

I shared an apartment with Kitty, another Australian nurse I had previously known for those six months. Helen Koutras' family and their neighbour,

Regina Finninger, were eager to help me to get ready for the upcoming wedding in Boston, which was to take place on February 26, 1976. The date didn't have any particular significance for us, it was simply the earliest we could manage so I could ensure I had permanent residency and would not have to go through the whole visa rigmarole again.

A new life in Boston

1975

I arrived in Boston at the end of January 1975 and because Peter had been living in the doctor's quarters at the hospital, I spent some time finding a suitable apartment we could live in together. We also had to do some fundamental furniture shopping.

We found a lovely, bright apartment in Watertown on the banks of the Charles River that was accessible to both hospitals we were working. Peter had already purchased his first car and was proud of his new 1975 Datsun B210.

Of course, I would need a car, too, so somehow, I bought a Fiat. When I purchased it, I had no idea what a winter in Boston would be like and was unaware of how Fiats would perform when the temperature was below freezing, never having lived in a cold climate. Indeed, Boston had four distinct seasons, which I quickly became aware of, and my car invariably

Margaret and Peter on their wedding day

refused to start without jumper cables whenever we had a freeze which was a regular occurrence in Boston.

We were married on February 26 without family as none of our relatives were in a position to travel halfway around the world at that time. We had twelve friends of Peter's, which was lovely and quiet.

There was no honeymoon, as Peter had to be at the hospital on Monday, so he could only be off for the weekend. After the wedding, we drove up to a friend's place in New Hampshire, but it was freezing, with very heavy snow on the ground and very little heating. Peter and I were half frozen trying to stay warm, which made it very difficult to get much sleep.

On my arrival in Boston, I was still under H-1B Visa status. Soon after we were married, I was in a position for permanent residency, which was granted a few months after our wedding. In the interim, I was given a temporary visa that allowed me to find work. I received my Green Card on July 15, 1976, officially known as a permanent resident card, which is an identity document that shows a person has permanent residency in the United States.

Green Card holders are formally known as lawful permanent residents, which means I could work and travel as any American-born citizen could, the difference being that I was not eligible to vote. Still, I was required to file taxes in the USA and if we left the country, I could not be absent for more than two years. So I was required to travel back to the USA for a few days every two years to maintain my status.

I chose to apply for a position in the Massachusetts General Hospital Cardiac Surgery Unit, as that was the field I had been working in. Affectionately known as Mass General, it is the third-oldest hospital in the US and was the original clinical education and research facility for Harvard Medical School.[11] I was in total awe of the history and museums and was pleased to be there.

One of the very memorable moments was accompanying a patient to the operating room for emergency bypass surgery when he had a cardiac arrest in the elevator, and I proceeded to do CPR. When he recovered, he was so happy and when he was discharged, he presented me with a beautiful watercolour painting. It wasn't until then that I discovered that he was the famous New England painter Robert E. Driscoll and his beautiful painting still has a place of honour in my home today, having travelled all over the world.

Peter was working in cardiac surgery ICU at Boston University and also doing shifts in emergency. He was studying hard for his Educational Commission for Foreign Medical Graduates, which is a certification for foreign graduates. He was studying and working long, long hours so we barely saw each other.

Alain Marengo-Rowe, our mutual colleague from Dallas, had come to Boston to attend a conference and called Peter to ask if we could meet him for dinner. Peter was on call at the time, so he asked if I would accompany Alain. It was wonderful to catch up with this old friend again and he chose to take me to Pier Four, which is one of the most beautiful waterfront restaurants in Boston. We knew we were in good company when we looked over at the table next to us. "That lady looks like Elizabeth Taylor," I whispered to Alain.

"Well, that's because it *is*," he replied. Sure enough, she was there with her entourage, taking in the clear night filled with stars and enjoying a delectable seafood dinner.

The city came alive several times in the year leading up to July 4, 1976—the bicentennial of the adoption of the Declaration of Independence by the founding fathers. Each celebration leading up to the anniversary date paid tribute to the historical events leading up to the creation of the United States as an independent republic.

A painting by Robert E Driscoll

I was still in Greece when the official bicentennial events began in Boston on April 18, 1975 with President Gerald Ford arriving in the city to light a third lantern at the historic Old North Church, symbolising America's third century.

Festivities around the country in 1976 included fireworks displays above major US cities and I was in Boston for the arrival of Operation Sail, a large international fleet parade of tall-masted sailing ships that had first gathered in New York City on Independence Day before arriving in Boston about one week later.[12] These were exciting times to be a part of in what was my new country of permanent residence.

Meanwhile, at Eurong, my parents were having a brush with silver screen royalty as the island was the location for the movie *Eliza Fraser*. This film, which was an adventure drama, was one of the first big movies made in Australia as it had a budget over $1.2 million dollars. English actress Susannah York and actor Trevor Howard were brought from the United Kingdom to headline the film, which was shot in Victoria, New South Wales and Queensland.

Although the film took a rather satirical look at the events around Eliza Fraser, the real-life woman's impact on the island was far from subtle. Eliza was an English woman who was one of eleven survivors of the brig *Stirling Castle* after it struck a reef hundreds of kilometres north of the island on May 22, 1836.

The eighteen people aboard were making their way back down to a settlement in Brisbane, but had no food or water, so made it ashore on the northern side of Waddy Point. What happened next has been incredibly hard for historians to determine.

Indigenous author and filmmaker Larissa Behrendt wrote in her 2016 book *Finding Eliza*, the Indigenous Butchulla people briefly apprehended the whites.[13] Eliza was taken off by the women, daubed with coloured earths and made to assist in the collection of food. Captain Fraser, who was with the men, died. Some of the crew—presumably in the second boat—made the remaining 220-kilometre journey to Moreton Bay and after fifty-two days, Eliza was rescued by a convict, John Graham, who himself had lived for six years with Indigenous Australians nearby on the mainland.

Numerous accounts of Eliza Fraser's ordeal have been produced, starting with her own *Narrative of the Capture, Sufferings and Miraculous Escape of Mrs. Eliza Fraser* in 1837, in which Eliza is portrayed "as a vulnerable white woman who finds herself among villainous black people". In some accounts Captain Fraser is speared while Eliza hides behind a tree, in others he dies accidentally or of his illnesses. Eliza describes the humiliations of being daubed and forced to work and claims to have been on the point of meeting a "fate worse than death".

One of the few *Stirling Castle* survivors, Harry Youlden, much later, published his own story, which disputed Eliza's version. Instead of being captured, Harry said he and his mate "were offered food and that the locals seemed concerned about their welfare".

Despite contention over the authenticity of Eliza's story, the island was renamed 'Fraser Island', in honour of Eliza's deceased husband Captain James Fraser. In June 2023, the traditional name of K'gari was reinstated.

It was clear from Dad's letters to me at the time that there was no political or historical talk about the real Eliza during the filming of the movie. Director Tim Burstall was much more interested in putting his Hollywood spin on it and turned Eliza into a comic figure.[14]

More than 100 First Nations people were flown to the island from Mornington Island to act in the movie and the film company appointed Dad to drive Susannah York—who played the titular character—to the movie set for the duration of the time the cast and crew were on the island. Susannah became great friends with my parents and was a frequent guest at Talinga Happy Hours, while my sister Jennifer would babysit Susannah's son while she was on set.

It was great to read that Dad was so excited to have a meaningful chore to keep him busy.

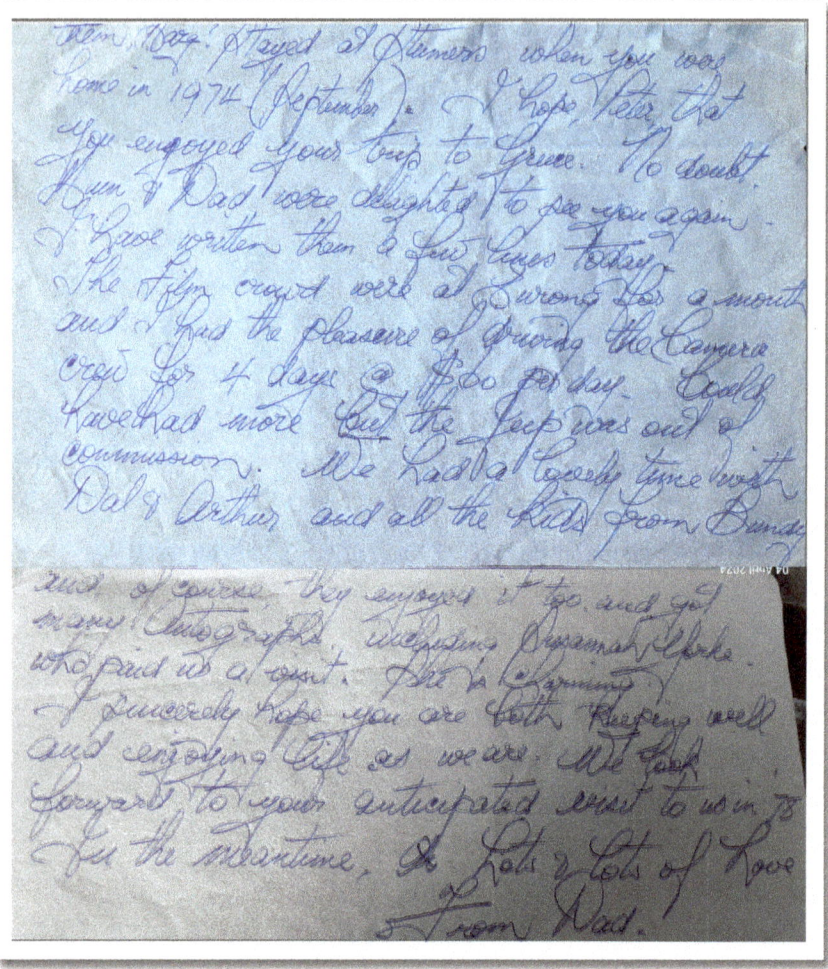

Charlie's letter about Susannah York, 1976

John's legacy

1976-77

The big news from Australia on New Year's Day 1977 was that my brother John had won the title of Australian of the Year for 1976. This was an annual award given by *The Australian* newspaper.

Seeing my big brother recognised nationally for his achievements was surreal. He had been fighting to protect the island with FIDO for six years at that stage and the group were making great headway in stopping major mining and other activities that had the potential to destroy the island's unique ecosystem.

John announced as Australian of the Year, 1976

Soon after that, John came to visit Peter and me in Boston. John decided that as the most senior sibling, it was his duty to check out my new husband, and from all accounts, it appeared that he had given my parents the thumbs-up on my choice of partner.

John and Peter had hit it off as soon as they met. Peter was amazed at how much time John spent at the desk in our second bedroom and never stopped writing every waking hour of the day and night. It was a habit that I was thankful for because even though I communicated directly with my parents over letters and cassette tapes, John always found time to keep me up to date with the goings on in the family.

Peter and John found that they had a lot in common as both were true pioneers in their fields of interest. Peter was highly impressed with John's amazing gifts and dogmatic dedication to win his epic fight for K'gari, which was not dissimilar to his quest as a Greek surgeon fighting for recognition in a foreign country. Hence they formed a very close friendship born out of mutual respect. I was so grateful to have these wonderful men around me, so that stimulated me to study and strive for more.

After several months of working in cardiac surgery, I became aware that the position of head nurse in the Neonatal Intensive Care Unit (NICU) was vacant. I was very interested in working with the great doctors and nurses, particularly in the research which our team of doctors and nurses were participating in at Mass General.

I got the role! It was a huge deal because I was a foreigner, but the accumulation of all of my nursing certificates, specialisations and years of hands-on experience in ICU environments meant I had a collection of 'strings' in my bow that no one else had. I was appointed as head nurse of NICU and also covered the Paediatric Intensive Care Unit (PICU) and held this position for almost two years.

I thought it would be a great idea to celebrate the lives of our young patients who had been so ill as patients and bring them back for a Thanksgiving Party, so the doctors and nurses could see the results of their care.

JOHN'S LEGACY

On November 19, 1977, I hosted the party, and it turned out to be a great morale booster and all the doctors and auxiliary staff willingly dressed up as clowns.

I was so proud to see this event take place and see the joy in the eyes of those great doctors and nurses as they interacted with patients who they restored to health. Such a rewarding experience for all of us!

A clown amuses a young friend.

Newborn ICU hosts party of thanksgiving for former patients

The sounds of children laughing and shouting often reached high decibel numbers, but no one seemed to mind. Quite the contrary! The scene was the Walcott Lounge; the date, November 17. Pediatric nurses from the MGH Newborn Intensive Care Unit were hosting a party to honor children who some time in the past five years were long-term, very ill patients of the Newborn ICU, and who were discharged well, after a great deal of treatment and care.

The Thanksgiving ICU-alumni party was a way of celebrating the good health of infants once critically ill. The one-time patients now range from less than 1 year to as much as 5 years old.

Attending were the children, their parents, doctors, nurses, and the allied health staff of the ICU. The partygoers were entertained by physicians from the Pediatrics Unit dressed as clowns, and by a visit from Santa Claus.

Though the nurses who gave the party shared in an intense and crucial period of their young patients' lives, most had not seen the children they cared for since the youngsters were discharged. So it was with real happiness that these nurses met the healthy children who were once so sick their lives depended on the resources of one of modern medicine's most sophisticated domains, the Newborn ICU.

Balloons, lollipops, and laughter were the order of the day.

The party was organized by Margaret Alivizatos, RN, Head Nurse in the Newborn ICU. Clowns were Dr. David Todres, Associate Director of Pediatric ICUs; Dr. Patricia O'Rourke, who has been appointed Chief Resident in Pediatrics for next year; and John Favarito, RN, of the Newborn ICU. And Edward Mackler, R.R.T., a respiratory therapist in the Newborn ICU, was deputized by Santa Claus to perform Christmas duties as the jolly man from the North Pole.

Mass General Hospital NICU party

Essential personnel during the Boston Blizzard

1978

On February 7, 1978, the arrival of the most destructive and fierce blizzard in US history brought everything to a grinding halt! The huge volume of snow, hurricane-strength winds and flooding tides resulted from two weather systems colliding and then stalling over New England. The first was a low-pressure system moving over warm Gulf Stream waters as it travelled up the East Coast. The second was a pocket of arctic air heading south from Canada. When the two systems collided off the coast of New Jersey in the early hours of February 6, a monster storm was born.[15]

It was a Tuesday, and I was off duty at home. Peter was at the Boston City Hospital working in the Emergency Room, and without warning, it became apparent that we were in for some really bad weather.

The storm came in extremely fast and within hours it was evident that it was not about to stop. In the next twenty-four hours, we had twenty-seven inches of snow, which built up on top of the base left by a snowstorm the previous week.

Our parking lot at the apartment in Watertown, which was about 8.5 miles from the hospital, was snowed under. The entire city of Boston was in

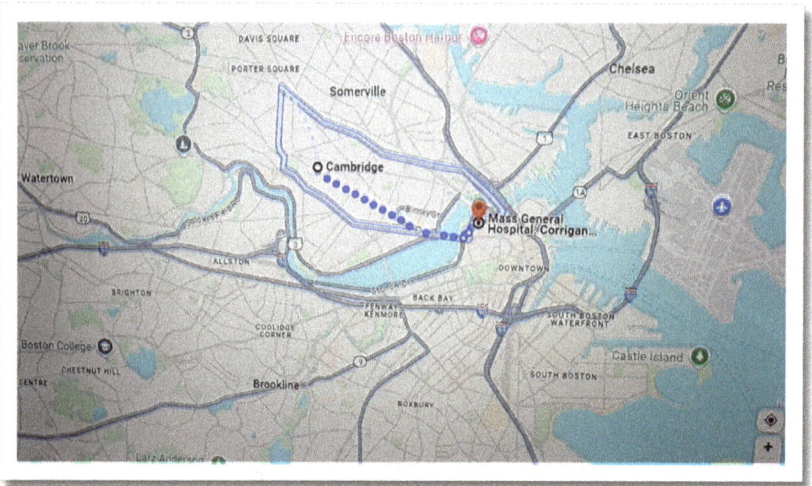

The train route to Mass General Hospital

emergency mode and involuntary lockdown as the whole road system was covered with as much as six feet of snow and entirely unrecognisable.

My staff in the NICU and everyone else in Boston were locked in their places for two full days, working with only those who had been in the hospital when the storm hit. Only emergency personnel and essential workers were permitted on the few roads that had cleared. As I was deemed to be emergency personnel, the police called to say they would pick me up from my home and take me to Cambridge Station, via the only road that had been cleared.

Only one train was running, and ran back and forth over the river to keep the bridge track cleared. There was a major problem; the train could only stop at indoor stations and had to continue through open-air platforms as they would not be able to get moving again on the frozen track, if it had lost momentum.

The police met me on a dug-out, eerily empty road and got me to the vacant station in Cambridge. It was an indoor station, so I could wait for the train to arrive and stop. It was usually a bustling hive of activity and it was unnerving to see it so dark and void of people. Once I was picked up, I sat with the driver, who informed me that when he signalled, I would have to jump off the train into a very high pile of snow near the Mass General station stop. He slowed down as much as he could, but it was still nerve-wracking to stand by the open doors and launch myself onto the snowbank as the train continued on without me.

As I exited the station, I saw a man who was quite startled to see another soul as there hadn't been anyone there for two full days. I'm still not sure why he was there when everything was closed, he could have been homeless and sheltering.

In 1978, Charles Street Station was on a high overpass with long, uninterrupted steps to ground-level. No elevators were working and when I got to the top of the stairs, all I could see was a long toboggan-like run to the ground. I could just glimpse the tops of the handrail through the snow. So, I sat down and slid all the way to the ground.

When I finally entered the hospital, I was greeted by cheers from employees who had not seen a fresh face for nearly two full days. They had simply scheduled the occasional sleep breaks on rotation and continued working.

Along the coast, flood tides forced 10,000 people into emergency shelters. Inland, over 3,000 cars and 500 trucks were immobilised along an eight-mile stretch of Route 128. By the time it subsided, the storm had killed twenty-nine people from Massachusetts, destroyed 11,000 homes and caused more than $1 billion in damage.

Peter recalled being trapped at Boston City Hospital, where he worked in the emergency room when the blizzard began:

> *Margarita, I vividly recall the blizzard with the snow almost reaching our back window on the first floor of our home on Riverside Drive, overlooking the parking lot. Our cars were entirely covered by snow and it took several days to melt. We did have a phone attached to the wall.*
>
> *We had beepers in the hospital and one called the switchboard from the nursing station. I slept on the floor in the Surgical Department for three days. The National Guard came daily, providing meals. It was great fun and a time of exhilarating camaraderie between staff of all ranks.*

There were twenty-some deaths on Rt. 128 due to people running their engines with car exhausts blocked by the snow, which was up to the windows. They had no escape as they could not open the car door to escape. It was tragic; the snow blocked the exhaust; thus, it was impossible not to inhale deadly carbon monoxide.

I cannot remember exactly how long it took me to get back home again, with Peter trapped at his hospital. It took at least a full week before work schedules and a sense of normalcy returned.

From Boston to Richmond

1978-79

The move from Boston to Richmond, Virginia was bittersweet for me. It was hard to leave my staff at Mass General, but on the other hand, it was a move I felt was indispensable for Peter's career. He had everything to become a highly successful general surgeon, but he wanted to elevate to cardiac transplant surgery and that would require a few more steps to achieve, and Richmond was one of the only two centres allowed to continue transplant research in the USA.

He was tired of all the study, which he had pursued with gusto for over a decade at this stage, but I knew he needed to keep going in order to achieve his goal. He had what I thought was the opportunity of a lifetime to work with doctors Richard Lower and Norman Shumway at the Medical College of Virginia, the medical campus of Virginia Commonwealth University (VCU), located in downtown Richmond.

At that time, cardiac transplant surgery had been on hold in the USA as the first attempts at human-to-human heart transplants had not gone well. Dr. Lower was part of the pioneering medical team who successfully transplanted a human heart on May 25, 1968, however the way in which the donor was deemed to be brain dead after suffering from a traumatic brain injury eclipsed the achievement.[16] It led to America's first civil suit for wrongful death and a focus on defining what constitutes a patient to be clinically brain dead as well as the implementation of strict protocols to secure permission from families of the brain dead or deceased for organ transplantation.

Despite the controversy a little more than a decade earlier, only two surgeons—Norman and Richard—and two facilities—Stanford University Hospital in California and the Medical College of Virginia—were approved to perform the necessary experimentation and develop the legal protocols before heart transplants on human patients could recommence. A major part of the research and development was completing heart transplants for animals in what was known as the 'Dog Lab.'

The opportunity to work with Dr. Lower was incredibly attractive for an aspiring transplant surgeon like Peter, although he was upset that his career advancement would mean I would have to compromise on my own. My posting at Mass General was very prestigious—one of the highest roles a nurse could have at the time—and if we were to stay together, I would have to leave to follow him to Virginia.

I was very excited that Peter had been given this rare opportunity, and I encouraged him to accept this fantastic work offer with another pioneer in cardiac surgery. I soon was happy that we moved, as it gave me many more opportunities for my own career that I had not anticipated. I secured the position as coordinator of the twelve-bed paediatric ICU and seventy-five-bed neonatal ICU at the Medical College of Virginia, the same hospital Peter was working at!

Sherlock and Margaret outside their apartment in Henrico County, Richmond, 1979

I remember having two weeks off before I commenced work and spent the time waiting for the removalists to bring our few pieces of furniture down from Boston. I spent the time getting to know our new environment and while I was in the shopping mall one day, I saw this beautiful golden cocker spaniel puppy in the window of a pet shop, begging me to take him home.

I had never even considered doing such a thing and had not ever discussed it with Peter, but he was so irresistible that I handed over $300, half of the cash we had in the bank, and took him home. I rationalised that I had about ten days to settle him and get him potty trained before I started working at the hospital.

That evening, when Peter came home, I presented him with the pup in my arms and was not optimistic about his response. "How are you going to take care of him while you are working?" Peter asked. "He will be fine, I've had dogs before and I know what to do."

Peter was not convinced, but we named him Sherlock because he always had his head down and sniffed, reminding us of the famous fictional detective Sherlock Holmes.

That night, Sherlock slept in the kitchen, which had a baby gate, and he was not happy and cried all night. The following day, Peter was furious; not only had I dug into our precious financial resources, but he couldn't sleep and instructed me to return Sherlock to the store. Of course, they would not accept him back.

So that was it and Sherlock won because we put his bed in our room the next night, and he was happy. Peter and Sherlock had a love/hate relationship for a while, maybe it was a male dominance thing… I don't know. But over time, they came to tolerate each other and eventually their relationship turned to love!

Soon after we settled in Richmond, Chris and Dee visited us from Shrivenham, England, where Chris had been posted while completing a Military Career Officer course. They visited us over Easter, around April 15, 1979, to introduce their three-month-old son, David.

Margaret with Chris, Dee and their children in Blenheim Park, 1978

Our two nieces, Karen and Julie, had grown so much since we met them briefly in England where they had been posted at Shrivenham. They loved playing with Sherlock and taking him for walks in the nearby park. We were impressed by how efficiently they handled such a long trip with three young children, particularly on long international flights. Looking back, I don't know how all seven of us managed in our two-bedroom flat, but we did!

⁓

Peter would share all of the exciting things he was doing with his work, and he told me about one of the Dog Lab heart transplant patients, called Terrazita. She sounded like a real character, so I went in to visit with her one day and she became a favourite to us.

Just a few months after Chris and Dee had visited us in Richmond, it was quite a shock to me to hear how Dad, who was one of the few people I had ever known to rarely be hospitalised or ill, was suddenly flown to Maryborough for medical treatment. I received a telegram from Mum to let me know what was happening, but she was stern that there was no need for me to hurry home as it would be too late.

Remembering Dad at Talinga

1979

On April 30, 1979, Dad left Talinga to be admitted into the Demaine Private Hospital in Maryborough. He had a pulmonary oedema cleared and Mum stayed nearby with John's family at 50 Queen Street. They discovered then that he had lung cancer because of his lifelong heavy smoking', and although he had been sent home on May 8, he returned to St Stephen's Hospital on May 22, and died on June 5.

I am grateful that he passed quickly as Dad was not one for sitting around. His funeral was held two days later, on June 7, and there was no way I could have made it back in time. That was another very traumatic time for me, but this time I had Peter and Sherlock so at least I was not alone.

Two days after the funeral, Mum returned to Talinga for the first time in her life to live alone. She had many visitors and little time to be lonely, but I once again felt so disconnected as Talinga only had the two-way radio and there was no way for me to reach her to talk.

Mum insisted that Peter and I stick to our original plan to visit Australia later that year. I felt so homesick, but I had my busy job at the hospital and Sherlock and Peter to care for me, so I just got on with the business. For the second time, I had to deal with a massive loss to what had been my family of seven, which had been reduced to five in the eight years I had been absent from Australia.

TALINGA

FRASER ISLAND REFLECTIONS

FREQUENT reminders of turbulent surf,
The ebb and flow of tide change,
Of dazzling sands and sea breezes,
All one complete ecosystem.

RAINFORESTS verdant and moist,
Towering under canopies.
Freshwater lakes,
Glistening mirrors
Perched in high dunes.

TRAVELLING NORTH,
Running the low tide beaches.
Sand dunes large and small,
Many more to explore,
SOFTLY we tread on sands
Long ago sifted by natures hands.
Everywhere we marvel the tranquility
Endless wonders of fragility.

KILO'S rolling over,
Navigator guiding
Maps strewn,
Calculators straining,
Time for a cuppa.

SNAPS of ibis white,
Brilliant in morning light.
Dingoes sleek and keen
Butterflies, spiders sparkling and clean.

CONSTANT wonder at the changing grandeur,
An amazing spectrum of colours,
Imprinting the urgent need to preserve
So the island may endure.

S. Bigelow

The late Charlie Sinclair taking the C.O.P.E. (Coastal Observation) readings for the Beach Protection Authority. The results of years of detailed daily readings appeared in the Government Management Plan released just prior to his death.

VALE CHAS SINCLAIR

Fraser Island has many well known characters despite its small permanent resident population. On June 5th it lost one of its best loved identities, Charles Prescott Sinclair, father of FIDO President John Sinclair, who had lived permanently on Fraser Island for the past 11 years.

Charlie's love of Fraser Island began during his honeymoon in September 1935 at Happy Valley which was then a holiday resort, and his love grew, particularly in the post war years. At this time he frequently visited the island when few Australians knew it or appreciated its significance.

After 40 years association with the Caltex Oil Company, and after raising five children in Maryborough, Charlie and his wife Beryl went to Fraser Island in 1968 to work at the Orchid Beach Resort which was then just expanding to establish the Fonofale.

After 12 months at Orchid Beach, Charlie and Beryl went to live at Eurong where they had built their house some five years earlier. While Beryl painted and showed her craft at Eurong, Charlie worked as a storeman in the Forestry Department at Ungowa until 1973, when he was forced to resign from the Forestry in one of the unhappiest examples of victimisation directed against his FIDO President son.

The irrepressible, always cheerful Charlie remained happily settled at Eurong where he was unquestioned King. Each day he held court on his back verandah, from where he could survey his whole realm. As many as 50 visitors per day from anywhere in Australia or indeed anywhere in the world, would come to visit. In return for signing the Visitors Book, they would invariably be offered a home brew (his famous C.P.S. Larger) or a cup of tea. His dogs Cassius and Pundi were his ushers.

He died aged 66 in his home town, Maryborough, after a short illness but his ashes have returned to the island he loved. He will be sadly missed, especially by Beryl, Cassius, and Pundi, for whom "Talinga" will be a lonlier place now. However Charlie has enriched so many memories of Fraser Island that he will not be easily forgotton by any who knew him.

An obituary for Charlie Sinclair in the FIDO newsletter

REMEMBERING DAD AT TALINGA

It was sad that we missed seeing Dad at Talinga and I would have loved for him to meet Peter. I know they would have enjoyed meeting after they had got to know each other through letters and tape recordings for the past five years.

We flew from Los Angeles and stopped over in Hawaii and New Zealand. In New Zealand, uniformed customs officers came on board without warning, with giant dogs on long leads that moved about the cabin, sniffing the passengers individually. It was a strange expereince unlike anything I'd experienced before and I could tell from the look on Peter's face that he was just as shocked. Clearly the dogs were checking for drugs, but once the cabin had been cleared, the officers moved up and down the aisles spraying us as if we were insects. I have no idea what that one was about... an outbreak of some sort?

Luckily things were much more normal as we carried on to Sydney and then the last short flight up to Brisbane. We chartered a single-engine plane to the paradise of K'gari and landed on the sand not far from Eurong village. Peter immediately saw how united the family he had married into was, and he fell in love with the spectacular castle we had at Talinga! It was wonderful to be with Mum and we could shed a tear or two together as we remembered Dad.

Peter wrote:

> *We landed on the sand, and there at the edge, Mrs Beryl Sinclair, a character taken from a Victorian novella, was waiting for us. Instead, on the short side and a little overweight, but with undoubted presence, she had an aristocratically rounded face and perfect English pronunciation (she was a teacher), not the rough Australian accent that reminds one of London cockneys.*
>
> *There was something theatrical about her, like a veteran actress. Her stage was now her home, and she moved around it quickly and gracefully. We stayed there for the next two weeks, and I barricaded myself behind the front room window, surrounded by a pile of books with the only consolation of the sea view.*

TALINGA

I had brought them with me because, at the end of November 1, I had to take the written exams of the American Board of Surgery to be qualified in general surgery. I was struck by the fact that the few swimmers, some enormously tall, fit young men, only splashed near the shore, and I wondered why they didn't go further out. Mrs Sinclair gave me the answer, pointing out the shark's fin in the open water.

Jet lag bothered us for the first few days. To get over it, we went for walks along the beach at 3am because it was summer in the southern hemisphere. We were accompanied by Pundi, the genial black dog that had belonged to Margaret's father. He had almost been torn to shreds by dingoes (wild dogs) that set an ambush and rushed on him like wolves.

Some wild (brumbies) ran free. I shall never forget Margaret's agitation when a male horse came up to her while she was sunbathing, covered in perfumed sunscreen, and it still makes me laugh. He had been aroused by the smell and her shame when she saw the photo I had taken is beyond words.

Our trip to Talinga was fantastic and Peter and Mum got on so well. Time flew and, on our way, back to the USA, we stopped see Chris and Dee in Canberra. We then went to Sydney for Peter to meet the Locke family before finally boarding our long flight back to the United States.

Peter's photo of Margaret with an amorous brumby at Talinga

Peter and Pundi

REMEMBERING DAD AT TALINGA

Beryl and Peter

Beryl and Margaret with
Pundi outside Talinga

Peter and Margaret after landing
on the beach near Talinga 1979

The send off party for Margaret and Peter's departing flight

New concept in nurse scheduling

1980

After we returned to our work in Richmond, it was time for me to take on a new project for the nursing staff; the development of the Nurse Scheduling System.

My primary responsibility as coordinator of the ICUs was working with two other coordinators to cover the staffing and nursing care of our tiny and very sick patients. With a seventy-five-bed NICU and a twelve-bed PICU, we had over 100 registered nurses to care for and arrange work schedules to cover sickness, leave and evaluations.

Soon after I had my feet back on the ground, I set out to tackle the scheduling issue and worked to invent a brand-new system that would allow constant coverage of the units and also give the nurses every other weekend off.

I devised a new scheduling concept that not only allowed for every other weekend off, but our nurses would not have to work more than four consecutive days and could look forward to a four-day weekend once a fortnight.

I was very excited when I came up with a simple and efficient solution by making Mondays, Wednesdays and Fridays always eight-hour shift days and Tuesdays, Thursdays and Saturdays were always twelve-hour shift days.

The schedule allowed for every other weekend off and nobody ever worked more than four consecutive days to get them on a forty-hour workweek. This was significantly different to the traditional five consecutive day, eight-hour working week.

I thought it was pretty clever. I'd never done anything like that before and it was highly successful and made the roster very easy. It took off after the scheduled was published a few years later in the *Supervisor Nurse Magazine*, which was the Journal for Nursing Leadership and Management, in February 1981.

Hospitals around the US adopted the practice and it is still in place in some to this day.

A New Concept in Scheduling for Nurses

A method of mixed scheduling was developed to help meet the needs of both nurses and hospitals.

Margaret Sinclair Alivizatos

The sick always will require twenty-four-hour-a-day care, seven days a week, without regard for weekends, holidays, or personal preferences. Although this is a fact of life, few student nurses are aware of what it entails—especially in regard to the actuality of working shifts. For a short period of time, many postgraduates will accept almost any schedule offered to them in order to work in an area and hospital of their choice. However, once the "honeymoon" is over, young nurses begin the search to find the "ideal" job that will offer their chosen specialty, acceptable hours, and ideal working conditions. Not surprisingly, shift work or scheduling are among the most frequently named reasons for discontent.

Staffing Patterns Now In Use

Traditionally, nurses worked a five-day, forty-hour week, with every weekend off. This system has not been surpassed for its cost effectiveness[1] or its maximum, consistent coverage of patients, throughout the week and weekend. However, increasing numbers of nurses now are demanding more free time to enjoy the pleasures of life. Weekends off are fast becoming one of the essential working conditions sought by nurses across the country. Nonetheless, institutions which have not yet changed staffing patterns to offer this benefit to employees have a difficult time justifying the expense at the present time when so much emphasis is placed on cost containment. Many hospitals found it necessary to offer schedules with every other weekend off in order to recruit new employees and to retain their existing staff. Some institutions have paid exorbitant sums to hospital consulting firms for advice in planning alternate weekend scheduling. To provide this benefit, many hospitals have been forced to function with "bare minimum" staffing on weekends even though some have excessive numbers of employees during the week. One increasingly popular scheduling method offers a four-day work week. The plan is functional if staff are scheduled for four 10-hour days per week[2,3] with some part-time employees available for additional help. Again, the disadvantages are the same as for the previously mentioned method: minimal staffing on weekends and big overlaps of staff between shifts.

Yet another alternative that offers excellent use of staff is that of the 12-hour day.[4,5,6] However, this method requires an eighty hour option, is fatiguing to the staff, and leaves an employee little free time on a work day.

In summary, it would seem that the best scheduling method is one which offers consistent staffing patterns throughout the entire week, is cost effective, does not require additional personnel, and is acceptable to the employee.

A New Concept for Staffing

With this ideal in mind, a new concept in time scheduling evolved. It offers the full-time employee a combination of two eight-hour shifts and two twelve-hour shifts per week, for a total of forty hours in a four-day week. To reduce fatigue, no more than two twelve-hour shifts are worked together with the longest stretch not exceeding four days (40 hours). The advantages of the mixed scheduling method are as follows:

(a) It requires the same number of employees as the traditional forty-hour, five-day-week, with every third weekend off, to give similar staffing patterns (see Figure 1).

MARGARET SINCLAIR ALIVIZATOS, R.N. is a native of Australia where she received her nursing education in General Nursing, Midwifery and Postgraduate Pediatric Nursing. Since 1971, she has worked in the U.S.A. as a staff nurse, team leader in cardiac surgery I.C.U. and head nurse of the Neonatal I.C.U. at Massachusetts General Hospital, Supervisor of Neonatal and Pediatric Intensive Care Units and more recently, Scheduling Coordinator at the Medical College of Virginia Hospitals in Richmond.

Margaret's nurse schedule as published in *Supervisor Nurse Magazine*, 1981

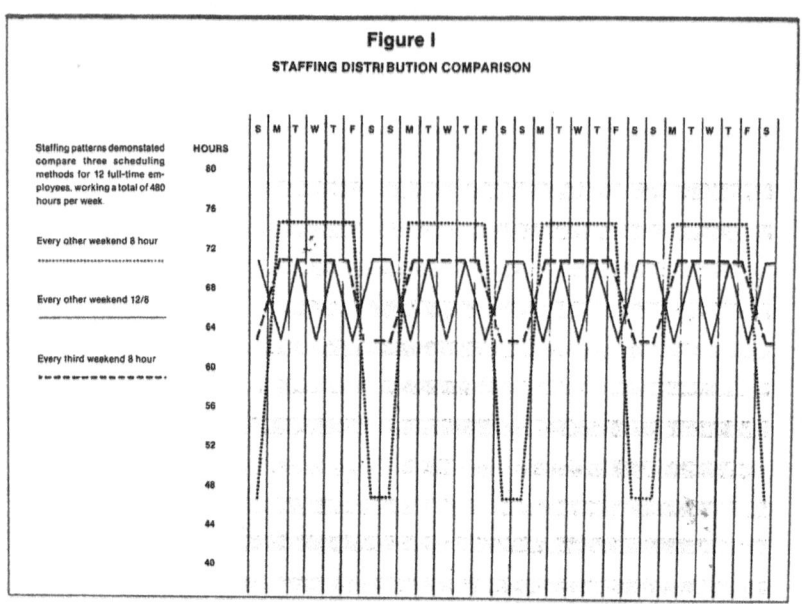

(b) It allows employees to have every other weekend off.
(c) It reduces travel expenses by decreasing the number of times the employee comes to work.
(d) It eliminates the necessity to hire additional part-time employees.
(e) It allows for equal distribution of staff throughout the week, including weekends.
(f) It is suitable for hospitals currently using forty-hour or an eighty-hour option.
(g) It provides flexibility in designating the day the work week begins (examples are given for the week beginning on Sunday).
(h) It lends itself well to cyclical time planning.
(i) It reduces the time spent in change of shift reports.
(j) It allows more time for staff inservices, meeting, etc., with more staff able to participate, especially on the twelve-hour days.
(k) It provides consistency in management if the Head Nurse works five eight-hour days with either every weekend off or every third weekend on to provide time with both weekend teams.

For ease in scheduling and to avoid confusion, twelve-hour days are designated by letters, e.g., $D = 7$ a.m. - 7:30 p.m; $E = 11$ a.m. - 11:30 p.m. and $N = 7$ p.m. - 7:30 a.m. Eight-hour days are designated by numbers, e.g., $7 = 7$ a.m. -3:30 p.m., $3 = 3$ p.m. - 11:30 p.m.; $11 = 11$ p.m. - 7:30 a.m.

A thirty-minute meal break is included on all shifts and an additional fifteen minute break is allowed morning and afternoon on the twelve-hour shifts; one fifteen minute break is allowed on the eight-hour shifts. To keep confusion at a minimum, certain days have been designated twelve-hour days

and others eight-hour days, i.e., Monday, Wednesday and Friday are eight-hour days and Sunday, Tuesday, Thursday and Saturday are twelve-hour days. Staff are not scheduled for more than four consecutive days, and will be given a three- or four-day weekend off every other weekend. To assist in planning of cycles, time off requests are limited to vacations, educational meetings, and special leave. Staff are encouraged to switch with another employee when it is necessary to change working hours.

To Determine Staffing Needs
Staffing needs are determined for any unit by application of the following forumla which illustrates a method used to staff a four-bed I.C.U. with three to four nurses needed for the 7 a.m. - 3 p.m. shift, three nurses on 3 p.m. - 11 p.m., and three nurses on 11 p.m. - 7 a.m. To determine the minimal number of staff required to adequately cover three shifts per day, the following formula may be useful:

Hours	Staffing
7 a.m. - 3 p.m.	4
3 p.m. - 11 p.m.	3
11 p.m. - 7 a.m.	3

Total = 10 shifts (multiply x 3)
= 30 (8-hour shifts per week)

7 a.m. - 7 p.m. (D)	3
7 p.m. - 7 a.m. (N)	3

Total = 6 shifts (multiply x 4)
= 24 (12 hour shifts/wk)
Total shifts required per week = 54/week.

Margaret's nurse schedule as published in *Supervisor Nurse Magazine*, 1981

NEW CONCEPT IN NURSE SCHEDULING

Figure II
6 WEEK TIME SCHEDULE

[Schedule table with 6-week nurse scheduling grid showing D/EA, D/EB, E/NA, E/NB, NA, NB, D/NA, D/NB rows across S M T W T F S columns for 6 weeks, with shift codes:
D = 7a-7p
N = 7p-7a
7 = 7a-3p
3 = 3p-11p
11 = 11p-7a]

To determine staffing needs for the unit, allowing coverage for vacation and leave, divide the total shifts per week (54) by 3.6 (i.e., 10% leave factor).

$$\frac{54}{3.6} = 15 \text{ full time employees (or equivalents)}$$

It is important to note that the "E" shift may be used to add strength in numbers at periods of the day when most needed. Figure I compares staffing patterns with three different scheduling methods.

Sample schedule, is made with 14 full-time cycles and provide 3 to 4 on the day shift, 3 on the evening shift and 3 on the night shift (see Figure II).

As 50% of the staff members are present on Tuesday and the other 50% on Thursday, this makes these days ideal for staff meetings and conferences. Staff are not scheduled for more than two shift rotations, either days and evenings, evenings and nights, or days and nights.

This method of scheduling has now been in effect in the Pediatric Nursing Department at the Medical College of Virginia Hospitals for 18 to 24 months and is also being used in several Intensive Care Units.

References

1. Rick, Kelvin S., "Alternatives in Scheduling Nursing Service," Durham, North Carolina, Duke University, March, 1972.
2. Scopac, Paul A., "The Use of a Four Day Work Week to Solve Specific Nurse Staffing Problems," Durham, North Carolina, Duke University, April, 1972.
3. Shaw, P., "The 10 Hour Day in the 4 Day Week," *Supervisor Nurse*, Vol. 9, No 9, October, 1978.
4. Crump, Kenneth, C., and Peter Newson, Implementing the 12 Hour Shift: A Case History," *Hospital Administration in Canada*, Vol. 17, No 10, October, 1975.
5. Cales, Alice D., "Twelve Hour Schedule Experiment," *Supervisor Nurse*, Vol. 7, No. 6, June, 1976, p. 71.
6. Bajnok, Irmajean, "It's Good for Nurses But is it Good for Patients?," *Hospital Administration in Canada*, Vol. 17, No. 10, October, 1975.

Margaret's nurse schedule as published in *Supervisor Nurse Magazine*, 1981

London calling

1981-84

Life had been settled in Richmond but as we moved into 1981, Peter started to get itchy feet again. He decided he needed more training in paediatric cardiac surgery. Being a perfectionist, he had to work with one of the world's leading and most recognised surgeons in this field and decided that Sir Magdi Yacoub in the UK was perfect.

Sir Yacoub had been the inventor of so many new procedures for congenital heart defects, which are problems with the heart's structure that people are born with, so he was the ideal teacher of this delicate specialty. This meant moving to London's Great Ormond Street Children's Hospital.

Because we thought we would only be away for a year, we decided it would be best to leave Sherlock with our close friends in Boston, as there would have been a six-month period during which he would have been in quarantine. Six months of quarantine in London was necessary because the United Kingdom is rabies-free. Since 1981, most countries have changed their quarantine programs, allowing animals to stay with their owners for six months under veterinary care approved by the receiving country.

We arrived in London in June 1981 and were able to live in the doctor's quarters at the hospital. Our new quarters were adjacent to the hospital and across from the village pub, which was most entertaining every night when it was the meeting square for all the locals, who would leave at closing time, singing and dancing. The location couldn't have been more perfect, and for the first time in my life, I was happy not to own a car as it would have been a burden. I got plenty of exercise every day with everything I needed within walking distance; the Russell Square tube station, British Museum, Oxford Street and the Arts District, so there was never a shortage of adventures.

We also had every possible venue for the concerts and arts possible, something we had both missed in the preceding few years. The two-bedroom flat was seconds away from the critically ill children Peter would be responsible for.

Until we arrived in London and I had assessed the situation, I felt it wasn't essential to rush into anything. I spent a little time walking and exploring before I decided to take a course in live art drawing at the gallery on Russell Square. While visiting Mum in 1979 at Talinga, I wondered if, given a go, I could one day become an artist. Just maybe some of her great talents had washed off on me. While living in the doctor's quarters at the hospital, I noticed an art school just a block away and enrolled. They offered live models, life drawing and oil painting.

I found the great photo of Dad and his dog Pundi I had taken when I was home from Greece in 1974. It was of him fishing at sunrise on the beach in front of Talinga. I found it a fitting subject for a novice budding artist and made my first attempt at painting since I studied art at school under the great teacher Alex Rotterveel.

The painting I created inspired by my photo of Dad and Pundi fishing at Eurong

Despite the painting becoming a treasured family art piece, I knew for sure that I was no Michelangelo and decided to enjoy the great art of the professionals instead of attempting to create my own. I was so disappointed that I didn't have Mum's talent and would never be able to survive as an artist that I decided to stop wasting my time and get on with the work I knew I could do well.

At the art school, I met a wonderful woman who was also destined to become part of my life's history. Jean Earnshaw lived very close by at Covent Garden, and from day one, we spent many great hours together.

I felt it was time to get back to what I was *really* good at—nursing. As an Australian nurse graduate, I had reciprocity with the UK, and I didn't need a work permit or visa in London, nor did I have to undertake any more exams, which was a relief. Interestingly, I would have needed all those things if I had done my training in the USA.

I chose to work at the University College Hospital (UCH) in London. Founded as the North London Hospital in 1834, it is closely associated with University College London, whose main campus was next door.

Because I wanted to complete the art course, I decided to work part-time for thirty-two hours a week in UCH Neonatal ICU, which was close to our flat at Great Ormond Street. I enjoyed living in that central neighbourhood, as I got to do a lot of walking.

I could relax a lot more as I no longer had the significant responsibilities of high-level management. However, Peter was as busy as ever and on call for his critically ill cardiac patients.

London was a great place to live and work, and there was never a dull moment. Less than a month after moving to London, we had another exciting event within walking distance of our flat. The whole city was abuzz on July 29, 1981, when crowds of 600,000 people filled the streets of London to catch a glimpse of Prince Charles and Lady Diana Spencer on their wedding day.

It seems that Prince Charles and Diana waited for us to arrive. Peter was working, and I left the flat to find a vantage point. When it appeared that I couldn't get close enough to see over the vast crowds, I decided to go home and watch it on TV from the comfort of my home.

Beryl and Margaret in London, 1982

Mum arrived in London in April 1982. This was the first overseas trip she had ever taken, and we were amazed at how easy it was for her to do it alone at seventy.

Mum and I spent long hours in the evenings watching Prime Minister Margaret Thatcher on TV, updating the country on the events of the Falklands War, while we knit sweater after sweater just because we wanted to knit. The Falklands War was a ten-week undeclared war between Argentina and the United Kingdom. The conflict began on April 2, when Argentina invaded and occupied the British-controlled Falkland Islands, followed by the invasion of South Georgia the next day.[18]

Three days later, the British government dispatched a naval task force to engage the Argentine Navy and Air Force before making an amphibious assault on the islands. The conflict lasted seventy-four days and ended with an Argentine surrender on June 14. Despite it not being an 'official' war, 649 Argentine military personnel, 255 British military personnel, and three Falkland Islanders were killed during the hostilities.

It was so much fun to have her with me away from her castle without having to share her attention with others. We bonded like never before.

LONDON CALLING

One of the highlights of living in London was the access to the arts and concerts, and we were fortunate to have Luciano Pavarotti at the Royal Albery Hall during Mum's visit. Somehow, we managed to get a balcony seat opposite the Queen Mother's box. She was in our line of sight for the entire show, but it was impossible not to be captivated by Pavarotti, who delivered one of his world-famous performances that evening. We were close enough to see the sweat dripping from his face as he wiped his brow with his handkerchief and gave one hundred per cent of his commitment to the songs he sang for us. It was so beautiful.

The trip to England was great for Mum, and she really enjoyed it. We had gone on the Scarsdale Diet—a seven-day low-carb and low-fat meal plan—and walked all over

The official Pavarotti show booklet

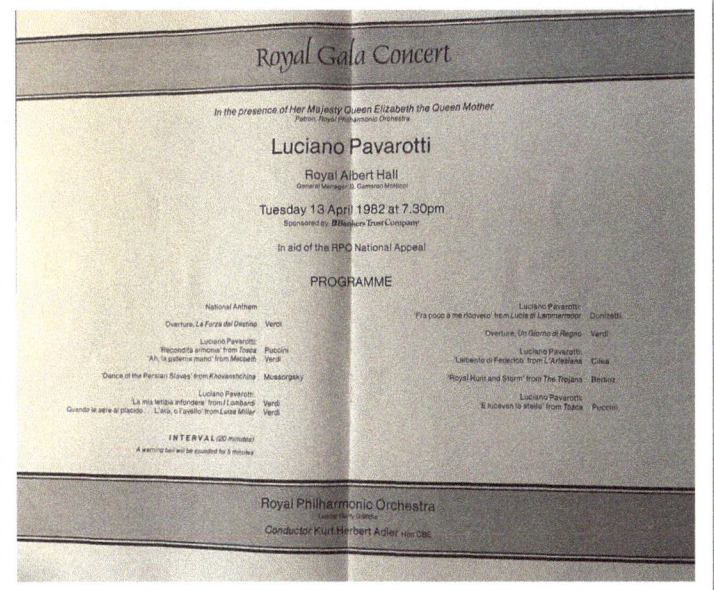

Pavarotti Concert London, 1982

town, so Mum lost quite a bit of weight. I think the family were quite surprised to see her when she returned home again.

At that time, Mum was transitioning from her home at Talinga to the granny flat Noel had built on his property at Bundaberg before he passed. He was a natural leader in our family and had the foresight a decade earlier to prepare a place on their block of land for our parents to move into when they became too frail to live on the island.

Through John, I had heard that Mum had reached the stage where she could not stay on the island as she had some medical problems and needed to be closer to medical care. Mum could live permanently with Dal and the grandchildren.

When our father died in mid-1979, Mum tried to stay on at her beloved Talinga, but daily life was becoming more and more difficult, being isolated from her family and essential health services. In 1981, her health eventually forced her to leave the island and move to Bundaberg to live with Dal's family. As Talinga was her only asset, she was forced to sell it and entrusted John with that responsibility. Selling property on the island in the early 1980s was difficult, and the family was generally reluctant to see Talinga lost to strangers. John solved the problem by forming a company—Fraser Island Holiday Lodges. The number of shareholders was limited, including those who love the island and several Sinclair family members. The arrangement demonstrated that people could acquire a holiday house on the island without each having a quarter-acre block.

The arrangement also gave Mum a modest income for the rest of her life. The company then expanded and purchased the neighbouring property, Weerona, a few years later. Weerona, had been built by my sister, Jenny and her husband, Ray, in the mid-70s and had become synonymous with Talinga. K'gari Holiday Lodges continues to maintain and manage both Talinga and Weerona, to this day.

I have always treasured this ode to Mum titled Beryl's Room which was written by her friend Sandra. It perfectly captures the way Talinga was when Mum had finished putting her personality into it:

Beryl's Room

By Mum's friend Sandra

Beryl's room was hardly bare! It was a kaleidoscope of crafts. Her home perched high on the frontal dune with a view that stretched from the lighthouse far to the south and disappeared in a haze of beach to the north. The house was not an imposing structure. It had started as a small fibro cement dwelling bath as a beach shack in the most choice (and most vulnerable) position, facing the full onslaught of the prevailing winds and weather. Over the years, additions had been constructed with a tirade of materials and the result was that all the outside walls, except on the seaward side, were new inside walls, and the original rooms were now converted into one living area, which became the hub of all activities.

Cakes were baked and meals were cooked in this room. Sewing, painting and other crafts started their lives here and spread throughout the house windows along the entire length of the wall that faced the sea, but there was no uniformity of style or sita. Some opened outward, some slid up and down and the louvres turned on their pivot point. Likewise, the window coverings were an array of blinds and curtains. Although the view demanded immediate attention and startled visitors when they first entered, the opposite wall intrigued and delighted the curious observer.

Every available space was covered with paintings, some partly hidden by wall hangings woven in wool and rope. The lights were adorned with macrame shades and baskets of ferns hung on ropes knotted together with sea shells and wooden beads. There was a low cane table in the corner by the old couch, which had started its life as a fish basket, been turned upside down and covered with marine pty wood, possibly all washed in with the tide Buoys and baits had been salvaged from the sand and used for decoration. Bottle green and bare glass balls had come adrift from the prawn trawlers' fishing nets.

In heavy weather, they drifted ashore to be collected and suspended from Beryl's ceiling, painted with wild horses, cut in half and planted with ferns and ivy.

Cupboards stood back-to-back at intervals across the room, defining the dining, kitchen and lounge areas. Each cupboard was cluttered with collections of books, family photos, and recipes cut from the pages of *Women's Day*, *Women's Weekly* and *New Idea*. A year's supply of magazines was stacked on the lower shelves for future reference. The whole room was a home, a collection of memories from the past and numerous projects in the process: sketches in charcoal awaiting splashes of colour, a tablecloth stencilled with wildflowers to be painted, embroidered, whatever. Lots of rope twisted, knotted, entwined, encircled.

I first did not notice the stairs, having come in at the 'other end'. An adjacent wall had been built to house a collection of shells and driftwood. The rails were hidden behind more art. When I realised that there were several more in this room, I wondered if they could hold more fascination than this buoyant conglomeration of the endless creation of art and craft that was Beryl's Room!

~

One must live for an extended period to get the feel of a city like London. I walked all over, wherever and whenever I wanted to, and in doing so, I became a beacon of fitness while having the time to take in sights of historic significance. With the London Museum just a block away, I spent a lot of time on my walk to work taking in Greek historical art that had somehow got to Britain (the Greeks say "stolen" some centuries ago).

Living in the heart of the city was a memory I will always cherish, but it wasn't without its dark side. There were still Irish Republican Army (IRA) bombings occurring in the 80s and one happened on July 20, 1982 in Hyde

Park, London.[19] Four Household Cavalry soldiers and seven horses who had been on ceremonial duty were killed, with many more soldiers and civilians injured. This was a little close to home, but it was a sign of the political unrest that still existed between Ireland the England.

Towards the end of that year, we witnessed another legendary performance at the Royal Festival Hall, London when Russian pianist Vladimir Horowitz returned to England for the first time in over three decades at the invitation of Prince Charles. He presented his most famous repertoire, including Rachmaninoff 'Sonata No 2' and Chopin's 'Ballade No 1'.

Schumann's 'Kinderszenen' also was performed in honour of the impending birth of Prince William. As Prince Charles was in attendance, Horowitz began with 'God Save the Queen', which brought murmured amusement from the audience.

I stood in line for several hours and got two excellent tickets right by the stage, where we could see Vladimir Horowitz's every facial expression and the close-up vision of his genius hands. He was eighty-eight years old and sadly died just six months later, on November 5.

As Peter's tour of duty at Great Ormond Street was coming to an end, he was offered a position with Sir Magdi Yacoub at the Harefield Hospital for another year. Since we were going to extend our time in London, we decided to bring Sherlock over. At the time, dogs born in the US had to go through quarantine to ensure they were rabies-free and did not transmit the disease to other countries that were yet to encounter the viral disease, which affects the nervous system.

We contacted our Boston friends who had lovingly cared for Sherlock and set everything in motion.

The Quarantine Station was a considerable ride into the country on the Tube; however, on my days off from the hospital, I visited Sherlock in his long dog run at least once a week until he was finally able to come home with us.

I never thought for a minute that Sherlock would be the catalyst for another significant chapter in my unusual life.

My first invention

1982-83

While working in the Neonatal ICU at UCH, I was looking after an infant who was one of the smallest babies. She had been born three months earlier at twenty-three weeks gestation, weighing just under a pound. She still only weighed three or four pounds, had a tracheostomy and was on a ventilator.

Premature babies have large heads proportionately to their bodies and at that time, there was no way to position their heads other than to one side or the other. I thought it would be much better for the baby if there was a way to keep her comfortable in a better position.

I had been on a visit to the quarantine station to visit Sherlock that morning. I took him a bed from the pet shop, which he was pleased about, and returned to the store to ask what was inside. They told me that it was a filling that was new to the market and gave me a small bag.

It was polystyrene beads. I had never encountered this before and, knowing that this would be perfect for my purpose, I returned home and created a design that would work for premie babies. I had a sewing machine at home, found some fabric and stitched it up quickly. The finished product turned out to be perfect!

I then had to figure out a way to sterilise it and asked the hospital's autoclaving department to run it through their machine to see how it would respond. An hour or so later, they called me to pick up my "pillowcase".

Jean with her dog and Sherlock, 1983

I then threw a handful of beads into a saucepan and boiled them to see how they would respond. When there was no change to them, I realised that the product could be safely machine-washed.

Excited as I was, I knew I would have to get permission from the matron to do a nursing research project to trial this new product with the premies. I was delighted when she said I could go ahead. I designed a report sheet for the nurses to record their comments on every shift and provided enough pads for every infant.

When the reports started coming in, it was a success. The babies were more comfortable and positioned in better posture. Another great outcome was the tiny premies had better thermoregulation. Their little flat heads started to round up and everybody was very happy with the cushion I had dubbed Premie Comfort.

As UCH was a teaching hospital, many doctors and nurses were visiting from all over Europe and requested information about where they could procure the product. I then made an order form, which was left on the unit, and within days, I had a handful of orders to fulfil. This response was amazing, so I filed a provisional patent in the UK.

Because the product was so new, I chose to go down the provisional patent route as it allowed me to add improvements over the twelve-month period. Then, with the help of my friend Jean, we began to make and fill a reasonable inventory of products to mail to customers. Jean was also a dog lover, and Sherlock and her lovely black poodle became fast friends and spent many happy hours together.

I had never done anything like this before, but I believed there was a healthy demand for such a product, and this could be a great help in caring for premature babies everywhere.

MY FIRST INVENTION

My beautiful baby, Sherlock, was my inspiration, and we set off on a new mission to improve the world. As things were moving along, another major surprise was about to change our lives.

Peter was working hard with Sir Magdi at Harefield Hospital with heart transplants and was in the epicentre of the industry innovation. The hospital is one of the world's largest and most experienced heart and lung transplant centres and went on to jointly pioneer the development of artificial hearts (also known as left ventricular assist devices).

However, in January 1983, Peter received news from Greece that his father's condition was deteriorating rapidly. He flew to Greece just in time to see him before he passed and be with his family to lay his father to rest.

It must have been heartbreaking to leave his wonderful, blind and aging mother yet another time. She sent him off again, her only son and heir, because she was a remarkably unselfish mother who had nothing but goodwill and wishes for her only son's future.

After his return to London, we decided that we were both getting beyond our reproductive years and with the birth of the world's first 'test-tube baby' in London a few years before, maybe we should try Invitro Fertilization (IVF) before it was too late. IVF was still in its infancy.

The concept of IVF resulted after a registered nurse, Jean Purdy, who was working with Robert Edward's laboratory, heard of the work of Patrick Steptoe, a gynaecologist who had developed a surgical procedure called laparoscopic tubal surgery with keyhole surgery.

In the late 1960s, Jean was instrumental in arranging the meeting between Patrick and Robert, who worked on the experimentation and protocols for ten years.

Margaret with Sherlock, the inspiration behind her invention, in London

The first IVF baby, Louise Joy Brown, was born on July 25, 1978, at Oldham General Hospital in Manchester, UK.

After my laparoscopy and two unsuccessful attempts in the very early stages of the procedure, I decided that a family was not meant to be.

In 1983, our introduction to IVF unknowingly coincided with my dear friend Gloria's husband, John Hynes and three colleagues setting up the first IVF private clinic in Brisbane, Queensland. Having received her degree in psychology, Gloria joined the group at their practice on Wickham Terrace to counsel IVF patients. John obtained his degree in obstetrics and gynaecology before returning to Australia in 1973.

Towards the end of 1983, Jake Lambert, our good friend and colleague from the Baylor team Peter had worked with back in the early 1970s, visited us. He offered Peter a position with the team to head a new team to start cardiac transplants at Baylor University Medical Center in Dallas. In March 1984, Peter decided to leave the UK and return to Dallas to start heart transplants with his familiar team.

Our next adventure was about to begin!

Texans once more

1984

On April 17, 1984, we left London; this time, we travelled on the same flight as Sherlock, who was accommodated on the lower deck in his crate. The eighteen-hour flight from London made a short stopover in St. Louis, Missouri, and landed at the Dallas Fort Worth Airport, which was new since our departure in 1973. The main airport in Dallas was Love Field.

On our arrival in Dallas, Sherlock seemed quite at home after his exciting world adventures. To our relief, as soon as he emerged from the plane, he was full of life and started to run with his nose to the ground with his signature Sherlock Holmes attitude.

We could take him directly to the temporary apartment that had been rented for us until we found a suitable home. I'm not sure what Sherlock was thinking after being shipped from Richmond to Boston, then flying to London and being airborne once more to get to Dallas. The weather in each location must have been somewhat disturbing for him, having gone from Richmond, where we had four distinct seasons, then on to Boston and London, and Dallas, where it was super-hot with about three months of winter. Then it went straight into summer for most of the year.

It had been twelve years since I landed in Dallas from Australia as a naïve twenty-eight-year-old single woman. Somehow, it seemed that Dallas was where I was destined to be. I eventually spent more than half of my entire life there.

It amazes me that I never had a say in where I would live. I never really planned my moves. I concluded that I was not cut out to be a planner like most people but rather a woman with an open mind who seized what I considered a great opportunity!

Some might say I just went where the wind blew me, but I think it was more like a direction from an unknown force. I have never had regrets, as I have been happy everywhere I have been fortunate enough to live.

- Decision #1: My first significant decision to become a nurse in 1959 was spontaneous when I visited the ER in Maryborough after a sporting injury—a decision made in less than twenty-four hours.
- Decision #2: To leave Queensland and do midwifery in Perth—a spontaneous decision made in less than a week.
- Decision #3 Accepting an offer when recruited to work in Dallas—a life-changing decision I made on the spot.

Little did I know at that moment when we landed back in Dallas just how much my life was about to change yet again totally.

Peter went off to work immediately while I took time to sort out our living situation. We both had to find new cars. Dallas was not a high-density city and didn't have excellent public transportation like London. After finding a car, it didn't take me long to find a lovely little two-bedroom house on Purdue Street, University Park, that we could move into as soon as our furniture arrived from storage in Richmond.

Peter voiced his opinion that I should not return to nursing full-time. I had a great solution; I wanted to make Premie Comfort available in the USA. I knew I could not continue in nursing administration if I couldn't commit to a full-time role, so this was the logical next move. It had been tested and the USA had a much larger population and many more NICUs nationwide.

I didn't want to waste time getting started, so once I was reunited with Regina Finninger and the Koutras family in North Dallas, I decided to find a patent attorney and file a patent application with the United States Patent and Trademark Office (USPTO) for my product.

While I filed it on September 14, 1984, it took almost two years to be approved on August 26, 1986.

Once our furniture arrived at our Purdue Street rental property in University Park and we had settled in, I took advantage of opportunities close to me. Peter was working with Dr. Ben Mitchell, who was the head of the cardiothoracic team. When I discovered Ben's daughter was a graphic artist, I asked if she could design a logo for Premie Comfort and a small brochure for the product to send to the 500 neonatal ICUs across the USA. She was amazing and had them ready in no time.

Meanwhile, I worked on a database of neonatal units and developed a mailing list. Once the brochure designs were ready, I printed 1,000 and made labels for the six hundred neonatal units in the USA. It was a time-consuming process to stuff the envelopes and mail them out. It sounds like a simple task for someone reading this book now, but sending out emails would have been much quicker. Sadly, the technology did not yet exist.

Regina and I went off to Fort Worth after Dr. Mitchell kindly loaned us his SUV to pick up some massive bags of polystyrene beads to fill our orders.

Margaret and Regina, who was the first official employee of Patient Comfort

With the material sourced and the sewing machine in place, we were ready to start making the inventory at home within a month!

I had cut and sewed the first several hundred of these tiny pillow casings and figured out how to fill and close them. Regina would join me a couple of days a week, and we were soon on a production roll.

The most effective process was to funnel the beads into each case, seal them up on the sewing machine, we would package them, and pack them twelve to a carton ready to ship to the hospitals. When asked if polystyrene beads were toxic, Sherlock ingested rather large quantities with no effects.

Within months of arriving in Dallas, I joined a local women's business group, the Association of Women Entrepreneurs in Dallas (AWED). They were a great, friendly group of women who had primarily established home-based businesses. Through this group, I learnt about the Cox School of Business at Southern Methodist University (SMU) and signed for their six-week course, Starting a Business, which was set to begin on January 1, 1985.

I registered Patient Comfort Inc. as a Limited Liability Company (LLC) and began operating Comfort Products from Purdue Street as a home-based business.

Meanwhile, Peter was beginning a new career as a fully qualified and highly experienced heart transplant surgeon, setting up a program for Baylor to begin as soon as they were ready. By the end of 1984, I had filed a second patent with the USPTO for Full-Body Support Pads.

Before the year was through, I applied for a second patent for full-body support pads or floats on December 18, 1984.

This was granted on August 19, 1985.

My new life as an entrepreneur

1985

I completed the SMU six-week course in Business Management for Entrepreneurs, which had classes one night a week. I took away the two most fundamental things that are necessary for any business owner:

#1. How to write a business plan.

#2. Long-range forecasting for at least three years.

Until that time, I had lived so much in the moment, making one decision at a time when situations and opportunities arose, that this was the first time I had considered the benefits of projecting many years ahead.

After writing my business plan, I could go to the local bank and request a $5,000 loan to purchase a computer

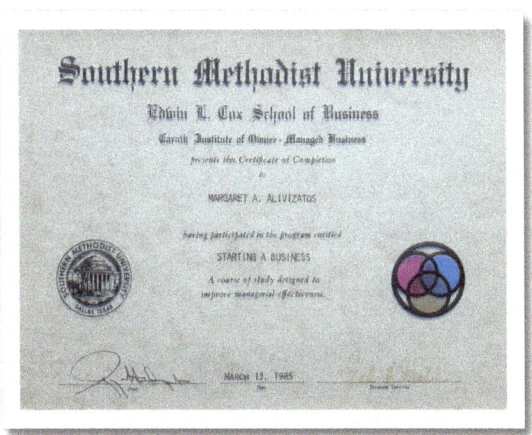

Certificate of completion from Southern Methodist University, 1985

and the necessary inventory to fulfil the orders for Premie Comfort that were beginning to come in and plan for future growth.

In 1985, it was difficult for women to borrow from banks without collateral, and women in business were relatively rare in those days, particularly in manufacturing. Even though I could provide the loan manager with my business plan and projected sales, it was necessary to have Peter, who was in a secure, high-paying position, guarantee my business loan. I must admit that I could not have got off to such a great start as quickly as I did without his support.

My first major purchase when I started the business was a computer. It was a top-of-the-line model with a 10 megabyte hard drive with Texas Instruments. It is hard to imagine now that even the most basic cell phone has more memory and power than my chunky computer in 1984. Microsoft began then, and purchasing computer programs other than databases was impossible. Very few people in those days had been taught how to use a computer, so I had to learn how to write DOS code and program my spreadsheets and database.

I needed to create a cost-effective business model and not lose so much time to paperwork. Initially known as the World Wide Web, the Internet would not be released to the public until April 30, 1993.[20]

Less than twelve months after arriving in Dallas, my business increased, with over 100 hospitals purchasing the Premie Comfort after receiving the brochures. Our one-in-six order rate from the initial mailout was very encouraging. I also began receiving highly positive feedback from the medical professionals using them.

With the company's fast growth, within six months, I was already outgrowing the home-based business, and it was necessary to move into a warehouse. I was fortunate to find a great realtor who was from Australia and had come to Dallas as a professional tennis player before developing a business in commercial real estate. His name was Ian Russell, and he helped me immensely in my search. My first warehouse was just 3,000 square feet. This allowed me to set up an office with a secretary and bookkeeper and, most importantly, sewing and cutting equipment to hire a seamstress to operate the heavy-duty sewing machines.

It was incredibly satisfying to see the business name on the signage on the front of my warehouse. We had a grand opening and invited many friends and colleagues. With the help of a caterer, we created a launch I could be proud of.

Margaret's friend Jean and sales representative Kathy in front of the Patient Comfort warehouse, 1985

My business was generating much buzz. Many newspaper articles were written about my innovative designs and how the products revolutionised infant care, particularly in ICU environments. Although Peter was on TV just about every day due to their groundbreaking work in heart transplants, it was interesting to see him become a little jealous when we would frequent cocktail parties or dinners for his work and more people started talking to me. I was no longer the quiet, supportive partner; I had established my path, and it was being noticed. Don't get me wrong, Peter was supportive and proud of me, but he wanted to talk about his work when we were out because that is where his passion lay.

~

Baylor had fancy donor dinners, and all the wealthy people who contributed financially to the hospital's research, equipment, and facilities would attend.

At one of those dinners, at the Grand Kempinski Hotel in Dallas, Peter and I sat on the stage beside a lovely man. We started a conversation, and he was so interested in what I had been doing in England that he asked many questions. We got on like a house on fire, with him asking me many questions about our travels. I had never thought to pick up the program on

Patient Comfort makes the Dallas Morning News, 1986

The Carrollton factory was basic, but functional

our table to see who the guests of honour were that night, but abruptly, the man excused himself and walked over to the microphone. He was the guest speaker, and it wasn't until he introduced himself to the crowd that I found out he was none other than the widely popular American journalist and TV anchor Walter Cronkite.

Wow! It's a good thing I didn't ask him any questions because almost everyone in the US knew who he was, and I had no idea until he spoke that night. Even though I'd lived in the US for several years, I hadn't watched much TV because I was so busy doing other things. In those days, we rarely had time to watch TV, with both of us getting established in our brand-new professional roles.

Margaret inside the Comfort Products office

Achieving goals

1986-88

1986 was a massive year for Peter and me. Peter and his team completed Baylor University Medical Centre's first heart transplant on March 6, 1986, which was a significant cause for celebration. The outcome was highly successful, but we seemed to spend less and less time together at home.

While he was incredibly dedicated to his patients, it was also a hectic year for Patient Comfort and Comfort Products, and I was frequently in the office for eight to ten hours a day and most weekends.

At that time, the full Comfort Products line included the Comfort Float, Cushy Comfort, Kiddie Comfort, Leisure Comfort, and Doggie Comfort.

It was a huge surprise to receive the 1986 Woman Business Owner of the Year award, which the Association of Women Entrepreneurs of Dallas presented. I couldn't believe I had achieved such prestige after only two years in business. After receiving this award, I was often requested to be

The 1986 Woman Business Owner of the Year Award from the Association of Women Entrepreneurs of Dallas

the guest speaker at events, including on protecting your ideas regarding patents and trademarks.

Sherlock quickly became a fixture at the warehouse and was considered the president by my employees, postmen and UPS drivers. My staff loved feeding and caring for him at work, and he went to work with me daily.

He knew the daily routine, and Sherlock waited at the front door every morning, eager to get going. He would race out the door once I opened it, and as soon as the car's back door was open, he was in.

By then, Sherlock had taken to wearing a child's size six tennis shoe because he had been injured and had a permanent arthrodesis of his left leg in 1986. This shoe was the only way to protect his foot. He managed his shoe very well and walked incredibly well without a limp.

Sherlock had a signature style due to permanent arthrodesis of his left leg

~

I grew my business rapidly by utilising direct mail and began attending trade shows for the medical industry and retail stores. However, my primary source of large orders was sales representatives for juvenile products and medical distributors, which necessitated moving to increasingly larger workspaces.

The Juvenile Product Manufacturing Association (JPMA) was a major annual trade show I attended as a member of my team of independent sales representatives.

The first significant account from the trade show in New York, Javits Centre, came when my nephew Greg Sinclair was helping me at the booth. Noel's son had flown over from Australia and was a great support at that show. Burlington Coat Factory, which had over 300 stores, placed a massive

ACHIEVING GOALS

Comfort Tote

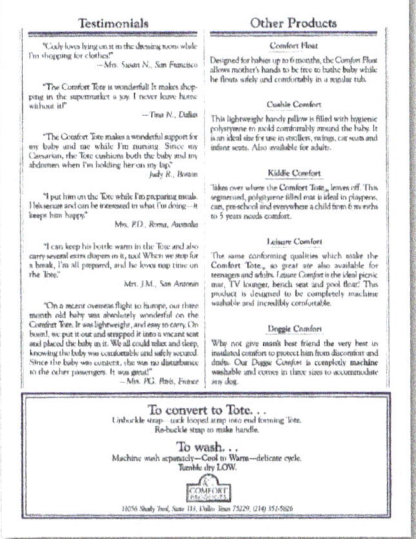

Comfort Products pamphlet

The Kiddi Comfort was introduced in 1987

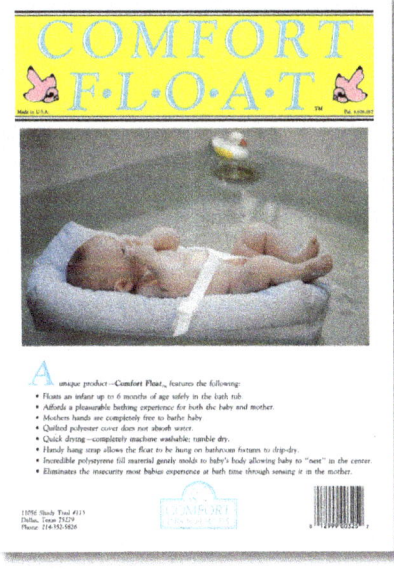

Comfort Float was released in 1987

order for the Comfort Tote at each distribution centre. Greg, accepted that order, which was dropped off just prior to the end of the show, while I was briefly absent from the booth.

After only three years in my original warehouse on Shady Trail, where I had grown from 3000 to 6000 square feet, it was necessary to move again. This time, it was to a 10,000-square-foot warehouse in Carrollton. My realtor was

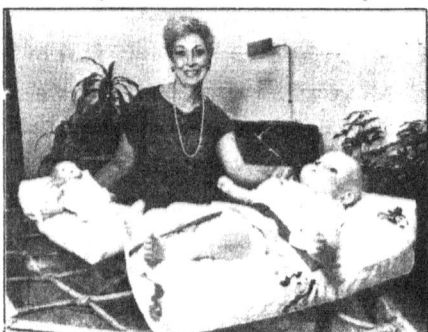

1986 Small Business Dallas features Patient Comfort

able to move me readily each time as he voided the contract term whenever it became necessary. This freed me up immensely to expand at whatever rate I needed and not have to sit under a ceiling due to restricted space.

Moving to Carrollton allowed me to purchase a boiler because it had much higher ceilings. This cut manufacturing costs significantly as I could buy the raw material and expand the polystyrene on site. The big boxes of raw material were transformed into polystyrene beads with steam, causing them to expand and form closed-cell foam structures. The beads are extremely light, so it was surprising to learn that the raw material was dense and incredibly heavy. We had to have a forklift transport the boxes of raw material to the boiler, as they were too heavy to move.

That would then be fed into the boiler to create the beads, and I developed a blower system to transfer the beads into overhead storage bins. At the time, nothing on the market existed that could effectively funnel the beads into a product like ours without having someone manually scoop them up, potentially making a mess of beads all over the floor.

So, I designed special plexiglass hoppers to deliver uniform measures of the polystyrene to the sewn cases. The hopper had two levels, so you'd keep the bottom level shut, open the top level to allow the beads to fall in, and once it was full, close the top level and open the bottom to deliver the beads into the bag.

It's a lot of equipment, but having it all on-site meant we had full control of the manufacturing process and could maintain quality standards and uniformity. By then, I had three full-time seamstresses to sew the product on three industrial sewing machines and a Merrow Machine to close the bags with a permanent seal.

My biggest problem was if an employee was ill. Being a smaller company where everyone had their special duties, it was easier for me to take over their duties until they returned. While this diverted me from big-picture management momentarily, it had the benefit of helping me to determine how to speed up production because I was at the coalface with the workers in various positions. When changes were deemed necessary, they became

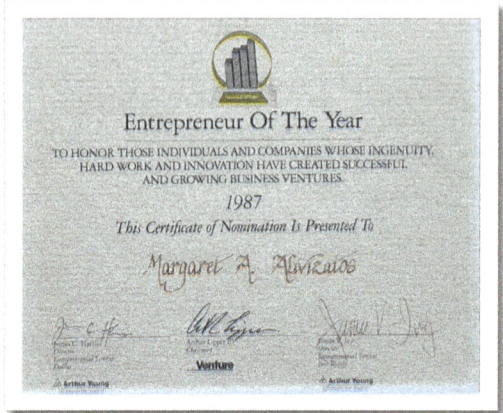

Margaret was named Entrepreneur of the Year in 1987

very clear to me when I filled in for my employees, and once they returned to their roles, I could implement the new processes to boost efficiency.

By 1988, I had to increase the warehouse's square footage to 13,000 on Champion Drive and employed ten employees to cut, fill, sew and package products.

My staff were beautiful, loyal and diverse. We became a little family, and my staff frequently stayed back on Friday afternoons to share Happy Hour and often helped mail out marketing materials. By then, I could print labels from our customer database. I had minimal staff turnover, and they all seemed to enjoy their work in my attractive, clean, airconditioned ambient with music playing most of the time, and it was a comfortably furnished environment.

I employed an in-house student graphic designer to create brochures and packaging. Realising photography would be a significant expense, I also invested in photography equipment and built a studio. The main problem at that time was that digital photography had not yet been developed, and it was necessary after a live shoot to get the film to a photo store and return for it to be ready, therefore wasting time and money.

I never had problems finding suitable models, but the photo shoots were tiring as working with small children and babies made for unpredictable conditions.

It was all worth the effort as I was nominated for the Entrepreneur of the Year Award in 1987.

Once the lease on our rental home was up, Peter and I purchased our first home, 4436 Edmondson Avenue, in Highland Park. It was a beautiful old home, built in 1924, with three bedrooms and a huge attic.

Mum arrived from Australia with my fifteen-year-old niece Karen on December 6, 1988. We were well settled into our home by then, and they stayed for Christmas until January 24 the following year. While they were there, we hosted a party for transplant patients and hospital personnel.

Peter and Margaret's Edmondson House, 1988

During the visit, they both came to the warehouse on many occasions. The number of patients who had successfully received new hearts through Baylor with Peter's team was growing substantially, and they were becoming a close-knit community. It was terrific for Mum and Karen to come to one of the New Hearts meetings to see the impact Peter had with his work. At that

New Hearts meetings were held in Margaret's warehouse. Patients are those wearing the colourful leis and others are doctors, surgeons and nurses

stage, the meetings were being held in my warehouse. I would do whatever I could to make it feel more homely whenever a meeting arose.

Several transplant patients connected with Mum and Karen and arranged for them to go sightseeing in Fort Worth. Their six-week trip passed quickly because there was so much to see and do.

The Juvenile Products Manufacturers Association (JPMA) trade show was held again at the Dallas Market Center in September 1989.

I grew a team of sales representatives to cover every US district, and they secured another huge order from Toys 'R' Us to ship nationwide. With the rep network, I never had a lack of sizeable orders to ship, keeping my shipping and receiving department very busy.

Orders came in from Disney stores, Baby Super Stores, Costco and many smaller retailers. We also sold fabric we printed under license, especially for Disney. I had to be well ahead of production, as much of the fabric I received in massive bolts had to be sent to the quilter directly from the manufacturer. I enjoyed having my fabrics printed as we were using so much, it was warranted.

Margaret (right) with sales representatives Kathy and Jackie at JPMA 1989

Margaret showcasing the Tutti Fruitti line at the 1988 JPMA

My farewell visit to Mum

1989

Less than a year after Mum and Karen visited, on Thanksgiving Day 1989, Mum called with news that she had just been diagnosed with malignant secondary cancer in her liver and informed me that she had opted for no additional investigations as the cancer was too far advanced. I desperately organised a trip to Australia to visit her and was able to return home in a few weeks.

Margaret with Beryl, Jennifer, Dal, John and nephews in Bundaberg, 1989

TALINGA

I made the trip alone this time, meaning Peter spent his Christmas alone that year. When I arrived, I was amazed to see Mum looking healthy and happy. She was living in Bundaberg with Dal and going about all her social activities as if nothing was bothering her, though I could see that she was in more pain than she was letting on.

Jennifer, John and Margaret, 1989

I could stay for a few weeks before returning to Dallas and was in touch with Mum as much as I could. She was always upbeat and told me of her activities, and then I received the dreaded phone call from the family just six weeks after I said my farewell in Bundaberg. She had died peacefully in her sleep after a heart attack while in the hospital on March 6, 1990. I was so happy that I'd had that time with her. I will never forget Mum in her beautiful Talinga, the house of love that Mum and Dad had built to give their family the utmost comfort and joy for the rest of our lives. She had a great life with Dad, and I'm sure she was happy to finally reunite with him after living without him for eleven years.

It is never easy to lose a parent, but now both of mine are gone. John was the glue that held us all together at that time. I was unable to travel back for Mum's funeral, but John, who always had a way with words, delivered a beautiful eulogy for Mum. This is just a selection:

Today, we would like to remember our mother and friend, who endeared herself to us because she never exhausted her passion for creativity, inspiration and achievement. But she had an additional virtue that distinguished her from the majority. At the same time, she practised her creativity in various forms, and she was never satisfied with less than a standard of excellence, which made her the envy of so many...

MY FAREWELL VISIT TO MUM

Those who have known Beryl Sinclair for her lifetime recall that once she had achieved her required standard of excellence in any craft, she would seek new challenges and turn to yet another craft and skill to perfect.

She was indefatigable in her determination to improve. It was an attribute she successfully transmitted to all her family members.

She marked her seventy-fifth birthday by winning quite a significant art competition here in Bundaberg.

Her needlework was legendary. She was an outstanding and competent dressmaker, but despite using machines, she went much further with her hand needlework.

Beryl had many talents and skills that always surprised even those who knew her well. This was particularly demonstrated with her keyboard skills. On rare occasions, she could be persuaded to sit at a piano or organ and play almost any tune on request with accomplishment, without a note of sheet music, provided that she had heard it at least once before.

Beryl demonstrated her creativity in her gardening skills. She made gardens bloom. She never lived anywhere without spectacular gardens. Like all of her passions, she pursued many facets of her creative gardening, including bonsai, indoor gardening, and floral art. In each, she achieved excellence.

Her most outstanding creative spirit, though, was in successfully engendering an intense sense of family. She created a wonderful, loving family of which she was fiercely proud...

Mum was never tired of rising to new challenges. She was always there when she knew she was needed. She was a help and an inspiration.

She inspired loyalty and affection from everyone who knew her. That loyalty and affection has caused us all to come from afar to gather here today.

TALINGA

> 4 Redmona St,
> Bundaberg 4670
> 3rd Dec. 1988
>
> Merry Xmas & a Happy New Year to
> Dear
>
> This year has been my year of travel. I returned from Sydney where I visited John & Sharan (John's new wife now) and my Brother Peter in Canberra. In February my dear old landlady, Mrs Henderson turned 100, so I had to come down to celebrate that. A week before Easter, an art mate and her family went to "Talinga", Fraser Is. with me and I stayed on for a happy and lively reunion with my Island friends over Easter. In May and July I had a week each time to see EXPO. (11 times altogether) I loved every moment of it. Hasn't Brisbane developed — what with Myer Centre and City Mall and the new Transit Centre! Cultural Centres!
> During the September school holidays Chris Jenny & Anthony, Karen Julie and David drove up to Talinga and I joined them for 10 days — another Island reunion.
> On Oct. 24 John & Sharan got married in Sydney and I drove to Sydney with John's sons. Later I stayed with Vicki (Noel & Dot's eldest daughter). Her husband Paddy is in the RAAF. She has 3 lovely children, my great grand children, Jason 5, Noel 2 & Danielle 1. I was there for Danielle's first birthday party. On my return, I went to appliqué classes & went mad on Aust. wild flower designs, so much so that I developed a market & demand for tops, blouses T shirts & work for fwrk panels. So I have made pocket money to help with my trip to visit Margaret in Dallas U.S.A. Margaret is shouting me my fare and Chriss eldest, Karen (almost 15). We are both wildly excited. We leave 10.30 PM. 5th Dec (2 days time) and return 24th January.

The Christmas letter Beryl sent to her family just a year before she passed from terminal cancer. It highlighted her personality and how vibrant and active she was

MY FAREWELL VISIT TO MUM

Next year I may settle down & live like a normal 76 year old. I have to return to my Art which has been a bit neglected this year what with my travels, patch work quilt and applique work.

I am now down at Jenny's & Ray's, getting ready for my departure.

All the family are doing well. Dal's family (minus Danny) who returned to Andora & London after 2 years away and a month back in Australia will all be at Bargara with her parents and sisters & families.

Jenny is busy as ever. This year she is back to Uni. to finish her B.Ed. They are all happy & well.

Chris & Dee are working hard at their newsagency at Moorooka. Their 3 lovely children are all doing well too.

I am in good health. My engine is wearing out a bit, but my wheels are very active still. I enjoy life immensely and have some wonderful friends in Bundaberg.

I hope this finds you also well and happy.

So a very Merry Xmas and a Happy New Year to you & yours

Best wishes from
Beryl Sinclair

Examples of Beryl's vast collection of her paintings (from 1960 to 1989)

The recall

1990

A few months after we lost Mum, I was called to an urgent meeting with the Consumer Products Safety Commission (CPSC) in Washington with five other manufacturers.

Because I'd had so much success with the patented Comfort Tote, several major bedding companies had decided to change my product design just enough to avoid patent infringement cases while reducing their manufacturing costs and selling to an even bigger customer like Walmart.

Unfortunately, as the original and only patent holder for the product, I decided not to file infringement lawsuits against the other companies. I rationalised that I already had the major juvenile product manufacturers purchasing the Comfort Tote, and I was therefore reluctant to spend $100,000 on a patent infringement lawsuit, which, in retrospect, I probably would have won. Instead, I thought it would be best to invest those funds in marketing to boost brand awareness and sales.

What I had not fully comprehended at the time was the impact of what these other manufacturers had done to make their product 'just' different enough not to be an exact copy. They had removed the straps, which were the feature that had made it an infant *seat*. They then advertised their products as pillows for infants to capture the massive Walmart market.

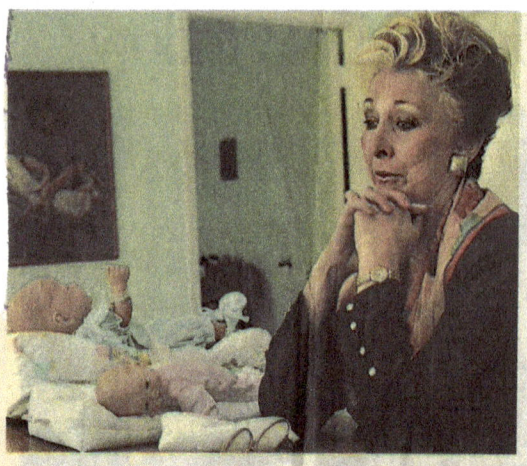

Media coverage of the devastating recall

Mothers started to see this style of product as a pillow and began placing their babies on it face down, which devastatingly led to cases of Sudden Infant Death.

At the meeting, I tried to convince the CPSC that my product had been thoroughly tested and used in hospital ICUs throughout Europe and the USA with nothing but paise. It was completely safe when used as a seat, which is what my product was. This was what distinguished my products from those of my competitors.

Upon my return to Dallas, I received a call from the CPSC attorney.

"Do you have an attorney?"

"No."

"You sure as hell will need one," he said and hung up.

THE RECALL

Safety agency overzealous, pillow manufacturer says

Tuesday, July 17, 1990 — The Dallas Morning News — 17 D

Continued from Page 1D.

The Consumer Product Safety Commission charged that the pillows conformed to the babies' faces, covering their nostrils and suffocating them in their sleep. The commission used a doll to illustrate its point at a press conference.

Ms. Alivizatos said the weight of a real baby, however, presses the plastic beads into a firm surface that does not conform to the face and nostrils.

"A doll is a very poor example," she said. "When a real baby goes on to these products, a baby with weight, this becomes very firm. It doesn't just come up and softly mold around like a feather pillow would. The polystyrene behaves totally different than anything else."

Ms. Alivizatos, a registered nurse, said the deaths are tragic, but not the fault of the pillows.

"It's the distribution of the weight that makes the polystyrene firm. There is no movement of the bead within the cover once it firms up," she said. "I still don't believe they've seen a real baby on the product."

The CPSC attorney, Mr. Moore, would not say if the agency tested the product with a baby.

Dr. Larry E. Balding, an Oklahoma City medical examiner who investigated the death of a infant found on one of the pillows, said the Consumer Product Safety Commission is using the flimsiest of evidence to draw its conclusion.

After hearing the initial reports of the CPSC warning, Dr. Balding began his own informal investigation. As part of his study, Dr. Balding bought one of Ms. Alivizatos' pillows.

"I'd never seen one of these pillows, and I thought, 'Well, maybe they are plastic-coated or something,' " he said.

The medical examiner said many of the deaths were linked to sudden infant death syndrome, which is believed to involve respiratory failure. "I don't believe that these pillows are causing infant suffocation," he said.

But Dr. Bradley Thatch, professor of pediatrics at Washington University School of Medicine in St. Louis, said the pillows "are very likely the cause" of the infants' deaths.

Dr. Thatch and an associate, Dr. James Kemp, are writing a paper on the pillow deaths. They say an infant's head forms an air-trapping pocket when sleeping face down.

Ms. Alivizatos' companies filed for bankruptcy after the CPSC action opened her businesses to possible legal action.

While the pillows accounted for only 10 percent of some of her competitors' business, the pillows were her main business. As an entrepreneur, Ms. Alivizatos personally guaranteed her bank loans.

Her companies' bankruptcy petitions in Dallas federal court are fat with $20 claims of individuals who destroyed their baby carriers as part of the recall. The handwritten individual claims are filed along with those of small retailers, seeking refunds for a couple of hundred dollars' worth of product each.

"They are all losers," she said. "They've lost their product, and many of them wrote letters saying how they loved it. But they don't feel safe using it when the government said it was unsafe."

Ms. Alivizatos' eight employees are now unemployed. And, because of the liability, she doubts she could be a principal in another small business. She does hope someone can buy her companies' assets and continue making the hospital and pet products not affected by the recall.

She began her business in London while working as a supervisor in a neonatal unit. She fashioned a bean-bag style cushion to support a premature baby at a London hospital, using a dog bed as a model.

She began making the cushions in her home. After moving to Dallas, she made larger cushions designed for transporting babies. The business grew, and she was named 1986 Woman Business Owner of the Year by the Association of Women Entrepreneurs of Dallas Inc.

Media coverage of the devastating recall in the Dallas Morning Herald

At that moment, I knew that no amount of fighting would prevent a total product recall and lead to bankruptcy for the company. The CPSC thereby announced a 'voluntary recall' of all polystyrene products for a full product refund to the retailer. Consequently, the retailers were to be reimbursed by the businesses who supplied them.

Within the first month of the recall, I refunded $100,000. For the remainder of 1990, I was consumed by cleaning up the disastrous mess left by the recall. The Comfort Tote was the only product in the line affected by the recall, but it accounted for ninety per cent of the income. It was a huge revenue loss for the company that could never be recovered.

It was pronounced that I would have to file for bankruptcy as I had obligations that could never be repaid, a substantial lease commitment, and employee payroll. I was heartbroken to have to suspend all ten of the employees within the month.

Despite the complete devastation of my business, I was also challenged personally when I realised how quickly your true friends are revealed when something massive shakes up your world. There were many connections I had made in the industry who were so quick to retreat, never to be seen or heard from again, but there were also true friends who never gave up on me and have remained with me through thick and thin. They are the ones who are my true friends to this day.

That was the end of Comfort Products—ironically, in the same year, it was poised to hit US$1 million in wholesale turnover.

Rising from the ashes

1991-92

The first day of 1991 arrived under a cloud, and I decided it was time to look for the silver lining in all that had happened. Hope came from Dr. Maurice Adam, Peter's medical partner, who believed in my abilities.

I first met Maurice when I arrived from Australia in 1971 while working in the Baylor University Medical Center Cardio Thoracic Intensive Care Unit. I looked after many of his patients following highly complex surgery. He was a very kind and gentle surgeon, and his patients loved him.

Little could I have imagined someday partnering with him in business. While his intervention could not save the original company, he decided to bail out my company and purchase the assets. In 1992, Maurice became a one hundred per cent owner of a manufacturing company, and I became his employee. I also agreed to repay his investment and pay him a higher interest rate.

Because Maurice had to figure out what to call the corporation after he bought the assets, we spoke about the kinds of products I was likely to focus on, and I said I'd like to stay with children's products.

We created Kool Kids, so he made the corporate name KKC Inc. The Kool Kids label was used for the retail market, while the Medco brand was for products for hospitals and nursing homes under the same KKC banner.

Maurice trusted my abilities enough to allow me to make something great again, so I created an entirely new product line from the same premises on

Champion Drive, utilising as much inventory from the previous company as possible. Although the assets were taken care of, I still had to honour the lease over $7,000 a month.

It was surreal to work in a 10,000-square-foot warehouse without employees. My only company was Sherlock, who was a little lonely without the great staff who used to make a fuss of him.

It wasn't long before I devised a brand-new product line for KKC Inc., catering to the hospital market under the title Medco and another for the retail market under the banner Kool Kids. When we filed patents, Maurice and I jointly owned the company.

My first new product design was a simple wedge that came in four different sizes and replaced pillows that were not as sturdy for supporting patients in a lateral position. They were named the abduction wedge, torso wedge, arm wedge, and lateral wedge. As soon as the patent was filed on March 6, 1991, I produced a video showing how hospitals could save substantially on their pillow and bedding costs while comfortably supporting patients in a lateral position, which aided in preventing bed sores.

In the meantime, I had very little time to do any home duties, and it wasn't until I hired a lovely old Mexican lady named Philippa, who did not speak much English and was a part-time worker, to help at KKC that I had any time. I also had her live with us. She would stay home one day per week and drive with me to the office with Sherlock and me for the other four days. This worked out exceptionally well for both of us until precisely six months after she started.

I returned to the office to learn that Philippa had left, saying she hurt her back lifting six-pound boxes. When I next heard from her, she had filed a claim for Workmen's Compensation, as she knew I had insurance. It turned out she had a history of filing claims, and when I spoke with the insurance company, they explained that it was less expensive for them to pay the claim than to file a fraud claim and that it was "just a cost of doing business".

At that point, I decided it should be suspected that if something seemed too good to be accurate, it probably was. And yes, my insurance was considerably increased when the next premium was due. After several months of the reorganisation, I could start staffing for KKC Inc., and I was fortunate that several of the previous employees could return to the new company.

Following all the negativity that year, I really needed a short break from it all, so my friend Regina and I went to France for ten days.

On our first outing the night we arrived, we decided to take the underground with some friends. It was fun and noisy, and when I went to pay for dinner, I discovered that US$1,000 in cash was missing from my purse. I spent several hours at the Gendarmerie the following day reporting the loss, much to the amusement of the police officers. I also had to get a new American Express card delivered the next day, which it did, much to my relief.

Margaret and Regina in Paris

After spending three days in Paris, we took the bullet train to Lyon, where we rented a car and toured the vineyards at Pouilly Fuisse and Meursault. After Regina attempted to communicate in her very exotic interpretation of the French language, we enjoyed being pampered at every restaurant we visited. It was a great vacation for both of us and one I will never forget!

The short breakaway was just what the doctor ordered, and I returned a new woman, ready to get going full speed.

In the meantime, I was seeing less and less of Peter as he was operating every day, and the transplant program was in full swing. The New Hearts Club grew weekly, and they were happy to continue their monthly meeting at the warehouse, which could accommodate their growing numbers. Sherlock had become their willing mascot.

As part of my product development, I designed the only infant bouncer for multiples in the USA because the product could be made for twins, triplets or even quadruplets if specially ordered. The standard lengths of PVC pipe were not long enough, so I custom-designed moulds with wood on a flat board so I could create 52-inch pieces of pipe and could bend the lengths as needed once they came out of the oven.

I found that traditional ovens would not heat the lengths I needed, so I also custom-designed a large oven. It was a delicate process because you couldn't heat up the ends of the pipe, or they would warp and be unable to connect to the fittings as needed for the design to work.

On January 7, 1992, a Patent was filed on the Baby Bouncers for Kool Kids, the first infant seat that could be made in single, twin or triple sizes.

I could also use the same moulded pipe for Medco products, such as the leg elevation frame, so they did double duty. It justified having an employee work an evening shift whenever necessary to fill the orders

One of the most lucrative products I ever designed was the Soft Split, which was filed on August 18, 1992, and this patent was granted on April 8, 1997.

At the time, if patients were combative or pulling out tubes while in hospital care, they were restrained by tying their arms to the bed so they could receive their care without interruption. I thought it was cruel and usually only served to distress the patient further when they needed the IVs and other treatments. With polystyrene being one of the primary materials

The Kool Kids Twin Bouncer

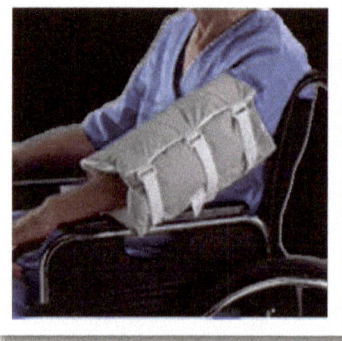

Medco Soft Splints

left in the warehouse, I started to think about how I could use it to overcome this common problem in hospitals around the world.

The idea of a split came to mind because it would immobilise the arm, and by using polystyrene, I knew it would be comfortable for the patient. We introduced the Soft Splint through Medco in 1992, and it was an instant success.

The Soft Split was made available in six sizes for infants to large adults and ended up being the most successful of all the patented products I designed. It was sold through several distributors nationwide, my biggest distributors being the Smith and Nephew Catalogue and the Sammons Preston Catalogue, which later merged.

On November 25, 1992, I filed a patent application for the second product in the Kool Kids line, the Baby Bather, a floating support for bathing babies.

The Medco product line snowballed, and by the end of the second year, I was spending as much time as possible attending trade shows and expositions, setting up distribution and training sales representatives. This paid off incredibly well, and it wasn't long before we were again filling sizeable orders daily.

I had not felt it necessary to patent all the lines and this gave me more

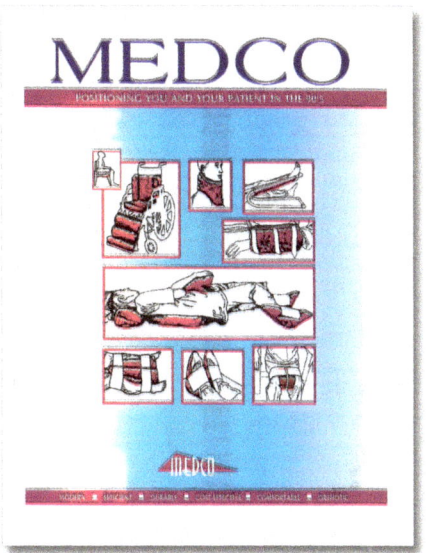

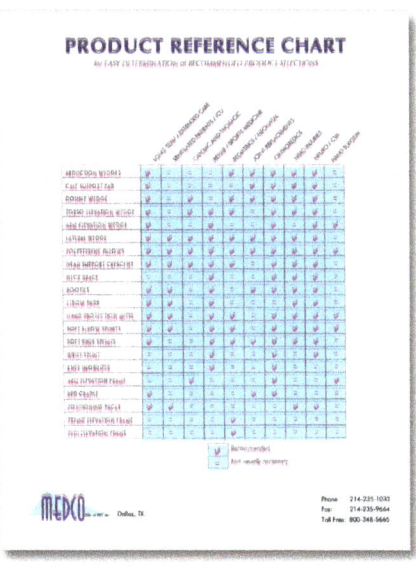

The full Medco line by 1993

freedom to see a need for a new product utilising common material we had in hand. Trade shows for Medco were totally separate from those for the Kool Kids, which meant that some years, I attended six to ten tradeshows per year.

I was travelling quite a bit of the time, and that was before cell phones were available, so I would have to stand in line at a show and wait to get a pay phone to call the office. When I was lucky enough to talk to my staff and had enough coins to complete the call, I would spend hours catching up with the office at the end of the day. It isn't easy to imagine how I ran everything before technology became an everyday part of business, but we did. A lot has certainly changed, with most manufacturing being done out of China now rather than in warehouses across the US.

While at tradeshows in the late 1980s, I began to see many foreign visitors, mainly from China, scouting the booths with cameras and secretly searching for new products to make in their factories.

Because my products were lightweight, bulky, and low-density, I figured they would not be eager to reproduce them overseas, and the freight would far exceed the cost to get the product to customers in the USA.

I developed the Kool Kids Before 'N' After pillow to accommodate pregnancy and newborns. It had a double wedge, so expectant mothers could lay on it to support their growing belly while side sleeping. When the baby was born, it could be used as an anti-roll pad once babies reached the age of rolling. The Before 'N' After pillow caught the eye of a Japanese customer who placed a large order. This customer initially had us ship orders to Japan but decided it would be best for him to manufacture the product in his country. So, he made a memorable trip from Japan to Dallas to my office to meet me, where he stated he wanted to buy the patent.

I did not think that this would be a significant product for the company in the future, and his offer surprised me until I learned that his wife was pregnant and that the pillow was exactly what she needed. I accepted the offer, and he took over the patent rights.

RISING FROM THE ASHES

The Before N After was snapped up by an international entrepreneur

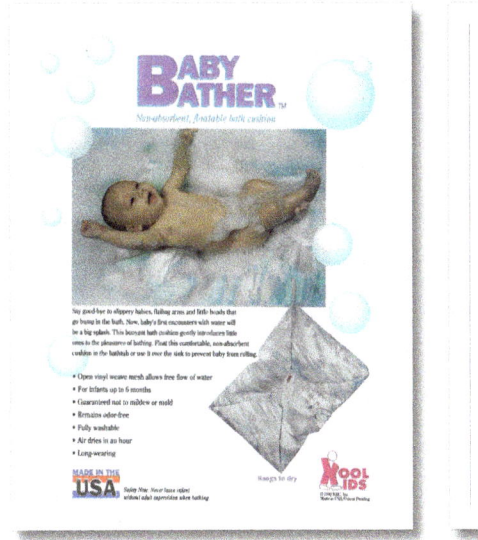

The Baby Bather was released in 1992

The full line of bouncers in 1993

The bouncers were selling well, especially in the designs for multiples, so I tried to find ways to innovate with the basic single bouncers. I had a bit of fun and created novelty shades in the form of the Fleurella, which had a die-cut large flower overhead, and the Baby Palm, which was very tropical with a palm tree design shading the baby. The latter became a customer favourite and helped to boost sales of the single bouncers.

Simultaneously, I had been designing a line of products for the aquatic exercise industry at the request of Sprint Rothhammer Catalogue.

Diane Rothhammer and I had recently met at a trade show, and she requested that I design a product for her catalogue. In essence, what I created for her was a repurposed Soft Splint design using outdoor furniture fabric, which we were also using for many other products. They were called Water Weights and could be worn on the ankles or arms. Their flotation created resistance and buoyancy and allowed deep-water walking. They were a hit with aquacise classes, and I used them myself when I went to my gym pool. I had the best-toned legs I ever had!

I had to have them ready for the spring edition, so I worked on sourcing new fabrics to align with their branding and felt the best place to do a photo shoot would be a tropical setting like Hawaii.

Margaret and Jennifer meet in Maui, Hawaii for a product photo shoot

Most of the products were simply the same cut and design as what was already in production, and all they required was a suitable fabric.

That fabric was already being sent to the factory, and it was perfect for its new use. That market was perfect for the company as it did not require us to take on more marketing costs, and we were ready to ship to the catalogue immediately.

Christmas 1992, I met my sister Jennifer in Maui, halfway between Australia and Dallas. We did a photo shoot for the catalogue and enjoyed ourselves immensely. There is nothing like combining business with pleasure!

〜

Back in Australia, John had extraordinary success protecting K'gari. However, his work had come at a tremendous personal cost, with many influential people working hard to discredit him and undermine the work he and the dedicated FIDO volunteers were doing. He captures all this in his book *Saving K'gari: The Campaign to Save an Island*.

In December 1992, K'gari was inscribed on the World Heritage List. Due to rising pressure, the Queensland Government established a 1990 Commission of Inquiry, led by Tony Fitzgerald, to recommend the island's future use, conservation, and management.

The United Nations Educational, Scientific and Cultural Organization (UNESCO) World Heritage Committee listed the island as Australia's tenth property on the World Heritage List in recognition of its outstanding natural universal value. The island's ongoing biological, hydrological and geomorphological processes secured the listing.[21] The scale of the rainforest vegetation growing on coastal dune systems on the island is unique. The world's largest unconfined aquifer supports numerous freshwater lakes, streams and wetlands, and K'gari contains around half the world's perched freshwater dune lakes.

John had seen the marvel of these decades earlier when he founded FIDO. His determination to protect the slice of paradise my parents had found as newlyweds led to the ultimate level of protection for the island. I was so incredibly proud.

The listing triggered a decision to remove the Fraser Island brumbies, as they could barely sustain themselves by eating the spinifex that grew on the dunes. They were an introduced species that was not native to the island. In the name of maintaining the preservation of the new World Heritage island, the brumbies were rounded up and relocated to the mainland. Unfortunately, some were culled.

The Goldman Environmental Prize

1993

I met John in San Francisco in April 1993 to see him accept the prestigious Goldman Environmental Prize, affectionately known as the 'Green Nobel'. Just three years earlier, he was recognised as a Laurette of the Global 500 as part of the United Nations Environment Program, and then he became only the second Australian out of the 193 recipients to be presented with the Goldman award.

It was the proudest moment of my life to see my brother, along with the recipients from each of the six world continents, honoured for being grassroots environmental activists. Seeing John's video presentation of his work on the big screen, along with the

The Golden Environmental Prize 1993 recipients: Margaret Jacobsohn Garth Owen-Smith (Namibia); Juan Mayr (Colombia); Dai Qing (China); John Sinclair (Australia); JoAnn Tall (United States); Sviatoslav Zabelin (Russia)

Sharan with John holding the Goldman Prize trophy

John with Margaret before the prize ceremony

attendees from around the world, was surreal. It was an honour to be present with John's wife, Sharan, and it is one life moment I have forever treasured.

John's award was a welcome distraction from everything that was going on for me personally and professionally at the time. While KKC Inc. continued to grow, the recall and ensuing business bankruptcy wreaked havoc on my marriage. I turned to Alain because he knew everything we were going through. He was an immense comfort, encouraging me to work things through with Peter.

This was easier said than done as Peter was busy with his work and regularly travelled to England to see Sir Magdi, so we had very little time together. On top of refunding all the recalled items, Peter and I had been served with a wrongful death civil suit as one of the families claimed it had been my product that had led to their child passing away. I was devastated to hear of any loss of life, but because this family had gone through civil rather than criminal court, they did not have to prove it was the product they had used.

Attorney bills came in left, right, and centre, and because Peter took care of all the finances, he signed cheques the day they arrived and became a veritable cash cow for the lawyers. Despite his payments, the problem persisted. I considered personal bankruptcy, but it was impossible while married to Peter. The stress was compounding, and Peter could not support me through it.

After giving my marriage much thought, it became apparent that it would be in Peter's best interest to accept a position he had been offered in Athens. It would allow him to return to Greece to be director of the new Cardiac Transplant Centre that the Christine Onassis Foundation had built. I was convinced that he could work for several more years in Greece, whereas he would be encouraged to take notice of the established retirement age of most surgeons in the USA, which was fast approaching.

This time, I wouldn't be going with him. I clarified that I needed to stay in Dallas to finish my new business and encouraged him that it would be best for us to amicably separate our assets and take advantage of this incredible offer to start a new chapter in his hugely successful life.

I firmly believed we could remain lifelong friends, and time has now shown me that it was a good decision for both of us. Our relationship began with mutual respect as I considered him the best surgeon and doctor I had ever had the luck to meet and work in the same environment. I also knew that I could never be able to share the culture and traditions that Peter had grown up with and something that was missing in his new life. I also knew that his parents and uncle wanted him to return to Greece after his lengthy absence from his native country. I'm sure that my mother would have been distraught over our separation had she still been alive, as she loved Peter very much.

The final New Hearts Transplant party at Peter and Margaret's home in Edmondson

Peter and I lived together for another six months, and we held the last New Hearts party at our home. Peter then moved into a high-rise apartment closer to his work in Dallas. I continued living at Edmondson Street and driving to the Carrollton business. The divorce went through without any hassles, and I wanted it to be an easy transition for both of us. Although I had supported Peter for many years while studying, he returned the favour when he supported me with my business ventures. I only asked Peter to pay the mortgage for the next twelve months until my business was more secure.

Sherlock's last photo, 1993

1993 was also unfortunate in that our wonderful dog, Sherlock, who had faithfully accompanied me to work every day of his life, suddenly took a turn at seventeen.

It was totally out of character when he remained in his bed and didn't want to come in the car with me, so I left him at home and went back to check on him after a few hours. Unfortunately, by the time I returned, he had already taken his last breath. Another death in the family was brutal to bear, and it was so sad for my employees as well.

John brought more happiness into my world right when I needed it. He had a memorable visit with Sharan, whom he had married several years earlier, to introduce me to Andres, whom they had adopted from Columbia.

Alain, whom I had been helping by redesigning his home by the lake, kindly hosted their visit. He instantly liked Andres and was allowed to drive the boat on the lake.

Alain had once again been a steady source of support for me during my separation from Peter.

We had always shared a similar outlook on life. We were both socially outgoing

John, Sharan and Andres aboard Alain's boat on the lake, 1994

and liked to be in the middle of the action. In many ways, Alain was the opposite of Peter. Even though he was just as dedicated to his work, his career had not become the sole source of focus for Alain as it had been for Peter. We became a unit and had Peter's blessing because he voiced his approval, stating that I had more common interests with Alain, who enjoyed little things like cooking and entertaining.

 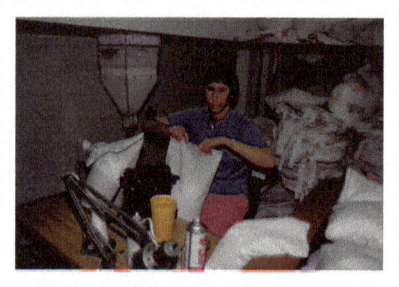

Margaret had great staff at the KKC warehouse on Champion Drive, 1993

Manufacturing was all completed on site at the KKC warehouse on Champion Drive, 1993

As soon as the law allowed me to own the company in 1994, Maurice and I were free to enter into a 50-50 partnership in KKC Inc. Business was once again booming, and employees had comfort and space. Employee turnover was very low, mainly because everyone enjoyed working together in a happy, stress-free, and comfortable environment.

It happened that the Carrollton lease would expire around the middle of 1995, and I would have to find a new warehouse. At around the same time, I had purchased a house in Lakewood that needed remodelling. So, I decided to find a smaller warehouse nearby, in North Dallas, to cut my commute substantially.

The new lease was just 6,000 square feet and had high ceilings to accommodate the polystyrene overhead bags for the business. Since losing the sales from the recalled Comfort Tote, I no longer needed the extra space, and my overhead costs were drastically reduced.

Designing Masinali Originals

1995

With a great product line and the manufacturing process now self-operating, it was time to do something more exciting with my work; medical products were doing well, and the Soft Splints had taken over the market enough that I didn't need to do more trade shows, as the distributors and catalogues had everything running like clockwork.

My cash flow was terrific since I decided that instead of accepting net sixty-day payment terms, which was the norm, I would offer my major accounts a five per cent discount to pay in fifteen days. My inventory was turning over at an incredible rate of twenty days, and the company had finally become an enviable cash cow.

This was wonderful and made me think it might be time to do something I had always wanted to do... move into fashion. I have never forgotten the experience

KKC employees celebrating the business birthday, 1995

of having one of my swimsuit designs copied in the '60s, and I hated the feeling of being powerless to do anything about it at the time.

For most of my working life, I needed to wear uniforms, which gave me little opportunity to be fashionable. It became evident that this was finally my time to create and sell my clothing line to retail boutiques. As I already had the seamstresses and commercial cutting and sewing machines, this was my golden opportunity, and my staff loved the opportunity to work with beautiful fabrics and finish the garments for my wholesale boutiques.

I already had a name for the line, which would fit perfectly on my label: MASINALI ORIGINALS. The brand was created by combining the first letters of my family and married names:

Masinali Originals

Masinali tags

MA = Margaret
SIN = Sinclair
ALI = Alivizatos

Next, I had to draw the designs, draft the patterns and shop for beautiful fabrics. I already knew the best places to source my fabrics, so everything was off to a great start. I also knew the marketing would not be difficult as I was just a few miles from the mecca of the World Trade Center and Dallas Market Center, where I had previously done many trade shows for juvenile products.

I wanted a comfortable and flattering line for everybody and designed clothing without form-fitting features. Aiming for one size fits all removes any juggling of producing different quantities of various sizes to meet demand. It felt great and simple, as I could also be in total control of the entire manufacturing process, while many of my competitors had begun to move their manufacturing offshore to China. I felt very comfortable with the simplicity of my designs and kept my manufacturing in-house, which proved to be great for my business.

My entire line was completely original, and when I went to trade shows, I would show the same design in different fabrics. The four-way duster was a huge success, as it could be worn four uniquely flattering ways and suited all body shapes. It was equally versatile for all seasons and many different fabrics. It became my signature item, and I sold hundreds of them at every single trade or showroom show.

Once I had designed the label for my line, I soon went into production to the delight of my seamstresses, who were bored making the same medical products one after the other because they could do so in their sleep by that stage!

Another of my signature designs was unique tie-wrap pants with an adjustable tie that fit several women of different sizes. It was an early favourite style, highly fashionable in the mid-1990s and far beyond. Changing the fabrics was necessary to transition from season to season and day to night.

In 1996, I exhibited the Medco patient positioning line and the aquatic line at the Medical Products Exhibition in Tamworth, New South Wales. I would like to arrange distribution in Australia. I quickly realised that it would have been

Masinali designs, 1998

The Masinali showroom, 1998

Medco Show in Tamworth, 1996

impractical to ship the cut and sewn shells to Australia, ready to be filled and delivered to the customer. However, Australia's population and potential sales were not large enough to justify the cost.

My social life blossomed with Alain. He was a licensed bare boater, which meant he could charter any boat without a skipper or crew. Usually, this meant yachts. During his two-week work holidays, Alain loved nothing more than renting a boat in the Caribbean or the Bahamas, and we'd sail all around Tortola and those areas.

Peter's return to Greece

1996-2000

March 23, 1996, was the end of an era for Peter, whom transplant patients farewelled at a reception in his honour on his retirement from Baylor. He was poised to move back permanently to Greece.

Three hundred people attended the function to honour heart and lung transplant recipients and families, and Peter commissioned John to fly from Australia as the guest speaker.

The audience remained enthralled as John eloquently shared the incredible story in his signature commanding, deep voice and described his fight to save K'gari.

John and his family returned to the USA for Christmas in 1997, spending time with Alain and me on the lake.

Because of John, I never felt neglected or disconnected from my family, who lived on the opposite side of the world. He visited us often and never failed to bring our family together whenever we could get away from our busy lives in the USA to spend a week or two in Australia.

As often as he could, John found the time to visit me, regardless of his busy schedule. He always took the lead and was very much the glue that held our family together after the deaths of our parents and my oldest brother, Noel.

In 2012, Alain was starting to have some health complications that came about as a result of his time in the military as a young man. He had been

John was the guest speaker at the 10th anniversary dinner of the New Hearts and Lungs group

Margaret celebrates Christmas at the lake with John, 1997

stabbed in the back while serving in Saudi Arabia as a British Army doctor. He had been attacked by an Arab and was bedridden for quite some time as he was unable to walk.

In those days in the 1960s, they didn't have scans, so he recovered in due course and seemed to return to normal. But thirty years later, in 1996, he had a CT scan as part of a check-up for suspected gout, and they discovered he was missing a kidney. The stabbing attack most likely had damaged the kidney, and it had then shrivelled up and been absorbed by the body.

Alain never had any reason to know he only had one kidney. It was a fortunate discovery as he had been on high doses of prednisone to combat his illness at the time, and this should never have been prescribed had his medical team known he only had one kidney. They were able to dial back his dosage and prevent his remaining kidney from going into failure from an overload of medication.

～

In Y2K, Alain and I decided to travel to Australia and arrived in Brisbane after our twenty-four-hour flight. Our visit was in May this time, so it was cooler and far less crowded.

PETER'S RETURN TO GREECE

After spending some time in Brisbane visiting relatives, I wanted to show Alain the island he had heard so much about and spend some time at Talinga. I hired a 4WD Landcruiser in Brisbane and drove north, calling into Pelican Waters to visit Jennifer and Ray before heading off to Rainbow Beach and up the beach to Eurong.

Having done this trip many times before, I did not doubt I could manage it myself. At age fifty-seven, I still had enormous confidence, and off we went!

The trip was pretty harrowing for Alain, who was driving in soft sand for the first time since he was posted to Saudi Arabia by the British Army with the Medical Corps in 1950. After getting off the barge, we made it to Talinga in one piece, and the first thing Alain wanted was a gin and tonic.

We hadn't even had time to assess the changes to the property yet, but with our drinks mixed and ready, we sat on the retaining wall in front of Talinga. As soon as Alain sipped the cold brew, he fainted.

It suddenly dawned on me that I was alone, and the noise from the waves crashing on the beach became deafening. I also realised that we were

Chris, Jen, John and Margaret outside Jen's home in Pelican Waters, 2000

Margaret and Gloria, 2000

probably pretty much alone in the village. I didn't have time for pause, so I started CPR, and Alain suddenly opened his eyes and sat up as if nothing had happened. All the nursing skills in the world may have been useless if this had been a heart attack. I would not have been able to leave him or summon help, not that there was any readily available anyway. At that stage, there wasn't even so much as a ranger station in town.

We still had the two-way radio on the wall, but I didn't know how to use it. In 2000, communications were still relatively primitive on the island and although we had cell phones, there was no reception.

Talinga in 2000

Once Alain was stable, we talked it through as medical professionals. We figured out Alain had experienced a vasovagal syncope (brief loss of consciousness) from the sudden ice-cold drink, and there was nothing more to do.

We had arranged for Gloria and John Hynes, as well as doctor and nurse partners, to join us. Having never been to the island before, they had arranged a flight from Hervey Bay to land on the old airstrip near Dilli Village, where I would meet them and bring them to Talinga. They were very much city people and weren't used to 'roughing it', but we had a fantastic weekend. There was a full moon, and we sat outdoors till the wee hours of the night, blasting Andrea Bocelli and imbibing fine wines and champagne.

Another lesson we learnt was that the solar panels could not handle excessive electricity use, which had been adequate for our first four days. However, when somebody moved into the neighbouring property, Weerona, in the middle of the night, Alain's CPAP machine suddenly lost power, and he had to sit awake most of the night. Fortunately, those managing the property were on the ball, and the problems were quickly addressed.

By 2000, I had a permanent showroom at the Apparel Mart before it moved to the World Trade Center in Dallas. The permanent showrooms were only open during the annual seasonal markets to bring in all four seasons. It was necessary always to plan the samples two seasons ahead. At the shows, one would take orders from the retailers with a specific advance ship date. It was the manufacturer's duty to have every order delivered to the customer.

Soft Splint infringement

2004

In 2004, I noticed that sales of my best-selling product, the Soft Splint, had unexpectedly started to level off. This was odd as it had been growing consistently for many years.

After reviewing the Sammons Preston Catalogue, I noticed one of my competitors was selling a replica of my patented Soft Splint. Without hesitation, I called the Sammons Preston Catalogue Company and advised them that the competitor's product violated patent law. I did not want to involve them in a lawsuit that I would undoubtedly win but that would be avoidable if they ceased to sell the infringing product.

Without hesitation, they returned all inventory to the Posey Company. Within days, my old friend Ernie Posey called me and begged me to enter a licensing agreement to sell the product. I advised him that this was out of the question and that I would not consider it too late, as he had knowingly infringed on my patent.

Ernie first saw my product at a medical trade show ten years earlier, when he occupied the booth adjoining Medco. I am sure that he could see that the Soft Splints

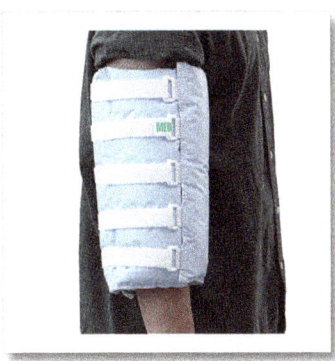

The Soft Splint design in 2004

would be a great addition to his product line. I exhibited the product at that trade show, clearly labelled 'Patent Pending'. He had nothing remotely like it at the time.

At some point, with my lease expiring the following year, I called him and offered an alternative to the inevitable patent infringement lawsuit that might suit both of us. I offered him the patent and the entire Medco product line if he was prepared to take over my entire inventory and equipment, allowing me to retire earlier than planned.

Ernie asked me to give him some time to consider the proposal and, within hours, called me back and asked me what I would accept. I suggested $1 million, and he countered with $980,000, as he didn't like working with round numbers.

I agreed and, within a month, had a contract drawn up by my attorney, which Ernie readily accepted. A few weeks after receiving the payment, Ernie had moved the entire inventory—everything except the office furniture—off the premises for ground transportation to his factory in California, including all machinery, fabrics, polystyrene hoppers, overhead bins, and packaging.

As I still had some months on my lease, I bought it out, paid each of my employees six months' wages and closed shop. This was a win-win deal for everyone involved, and what initially seemed like a significant problem benefitted everyone.

Nothing in the business world will be like a great win-win deal!

The Soft Splint, bought out by the Posey Company in 2005, remains available to the medical supply industry. As of 2025, ALIMED still sells it in six sizes under Posey.

Out of my seven patents for medical use, the Soft Splint has been one of my most successful. It has been available since it was first designed in 1992 and has now been commercially available for over thirty-three years.

The sale of Medco was made even sweeter as it allowed me to clear my debt to Maurice. My greatest pleasure was when I could finally pay off his entire capital investment and personally deliver him a bank check

SOFT SPLINT INFRINGEMENT

 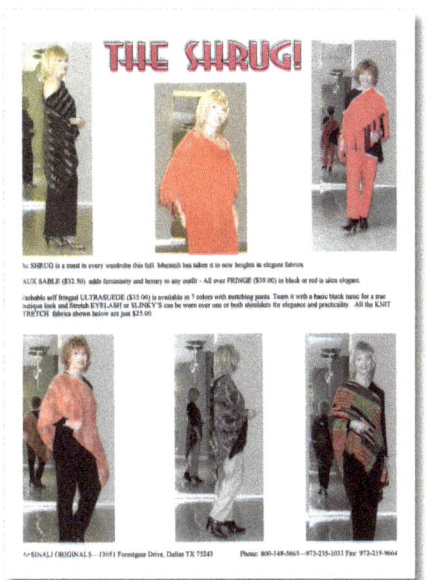

Masinali Originals brochure

for over US$300,000, which became possible because of the sale to the Posey Company.

Sadly, the sale came just a few months before Maurice passed away in early 2005.

Unfortunately, I no longer had my manufacturing facility and staff available, as the sales from Masinali were inadequate to finance the in-house manufacturing that had made it possible. I went to one final show with my designs. With the sale of Medco, KKC Inc.'s mother company, I would lose all my manufacturing capabilities, as it was part of the sales agreement.

I was in a position to take care of my faithful employees, and I paid them all six months' wages. It was no fault of theirs that they no longer had work, and for most of them, they were the sole providers to their families.

First attempt at retirement

2005

I was sixty-two when the Soft Splint patent and Medco business was sold to KKC Inc.

Alain was also retired and free from his medical obligations. In the final years of his career, Alain was an expert witness for drug companies, working with companies like Roche Pharmaceuticals Johnson & Johnson and many more.

Anyone in the medical field who had to defend their companies in court cases sought him out. He always won for them because he was a great scholar and knew medicine backwards. He was one of the best doctors I've ever met. If someone had an ache or a pain, without any testing and just a very detailed evaluation, Alain was never wrong in his final diagnosis. He was a brilliant physician.

I had helped Alain rebuild his lake house by designing the perfect layout to allow him to live in it if his health became an issue. As the house was finally

Alain and Margaret in Currimundi, 2006

TALINGA

Alain, Margaret and Peter in Greece

Peter and Alain reunite

Alain and Margaret with family in Provence, 2006

completed, I encouraged him to visit his cousins in France, his brother in Scotland, and his sister in Italy.

As he had always been his happiest while smelling the ocean and feeling the sand between his toes, I decided to invest in a house in Australia, where I still planned to return regularly. I chose a home on Currimundi Lake on the Sunshine Coast, close to Jen and Dal and not far from Brisbane, where several other relatives resided. This location allowed us to return to Australia several months each year and travel to Europe to visit Alain's family for one month each year.

I also sold my Lakewood home and invested in a smaller condominium at the Renaissance on Turtle Creek in Dallas, where we could spend time when we weren't at Alain's house at Cedar Creek, just an hour's drive from Dallas.

It felt incredible that I no longer had the responsibilities of business ownership. Born to British parents, Alain grew up in Egypt and loved the desert climate.

We could also spend at least one month in Europe every year in a different region within France or Italy. It became our responsibility to rent a five-bedroom villa with a swimming pool while the cousins would arrange our transportation. This arrangement was perfect for all of us and allowed us to live like the locals, attend the local markets, and take turns cooking or checking out the local restaurants.

Another thing we were able to do while 'retired' was to take advantage of cruising with our dear friends, Sara Lee Goff and her close friend, Don. I met Sara Lee, who owned a highly successful business in Dallas with multiple stores, through Masinali Originals when she purchased some outfits from my showroom. She and Don became regular dinner partners at each other's homes and travelled on several cruises to the Panama Canal and some transatlantic trips to the Mediterranean.

During one of these trips, we were met by Peter, who picked us up from the terminal in Piraeus and took us to a most beautiful restaurant for lunch in the hills with a superb view.

Peter had visited us at the lake house earlier, and we had a wonderful time meeting his girlfriend over lunch. Peter and I went upstairs to Alain's study when Peter said, "You know, you made the right decision with Alain. You're having a much better life with him than I ever could have given you."

It was so lovely to hear those words. Peter had always condoned our relationship, but in a small way, this was Peter acknowledging that he was all work, no play and Alain was a better match for me.

Once Alain and I had no work commitments, we could travel the world like others.

JJ's arrival

2008

John called with wonderful news—on May 21, 2007, the island became one of fifteen World Heritage places included in the National Heritage List. Australia's national heritage list comprises exceptional natural and cultural places that contribute to the country's identity. By that stage, the cultural significance of K'gari was being valued as highly as its natural features.

Back in the US, Alain and I expanded our family with the arrival of a four-legged friend. It all started with my seamstress' dog, Jazzy. We had been asked to look after Jazzy as my seamstress was from Germany and had gone back to be closer to family.

Like Sherlock, Jazzy had become a four-legged honorary staff member, and I couldn't bear the thought of anything happening to Jazzy if a suitable home could not be found.

He was an absolutely lovely dog, and Gloria was able to meet him when she and John came to visit us at the lake house. Jazzy came out on the boat with the four of us during that visit, and as we were coming back into the dock, he must have been in a hurry to go to the toilet because he jumped onto the concrete dock rather than waiting for us to tie up.

He just missed landing, fell into the water and went under the boat. I couldn't breathe as we all scrambled around in a panic. Jazzy surfaced and seemed okay as he resurfaced and swam onto dry land. While he made it up without a fuss, Jazzy let out this terrible howl and lay down once he started walking.

Of course, these things always happen on a weekend, and there was no one we could take him to until the veterinary clinic opened again on Monday. It was clear he was in pain, so it wasn't perfect, but with two doctors and two nurses in the house, we did our best to care for him and keep him comfortable. We were on the vet's doorstep first thing on Monday, and they wanted us to leave him there to undergo examinations to see what the extent of his injuries were. I didn't get to see Jazzy again before he passed. The vet called to let us know they had lost him, but they still did not have any answers.

"I don't understand why, but I'd like to do a post-mortem," the vet said. We agreed.

They found that Jazzy's bladder had ruptured as a result of the impact against the dock. The vet also saw a big stone in his bladder, which would have compounded the issue. I was devastated to lose Jazzy and told Alain there was no way I would ever get another dog because losing them was too painful.

The following week, our plumber called me to say there was a sign up at the local vet for 'cockapoos' for sale. The cocker spaniel/poodle mixes were so incredibly cute, and though I'd said I didn't want another dog, Alain and I went down to look at the puppies.

The owners met us in their utility, and there were three little puppies. A white male puppy sat in the middle, with a sister on either side biting his ears. Alain said, "Oh! I can't let that keep happening to him!"

He was so gorgeous and my heart melted. Everyone says you shouldn't take the most subdued, quiet one and instead take the active ones home, but we took him there and then!

We called him JJ, which was short for Jazzy Junior. I honestly could not think of a name! JJ was a beautiful dog, the only one I had ever known who loved balloons. We had a party for Alain's seventy-fifth birthday at the lake house, and I filled a room with helium balloons. We had twenty-seven-foot

JJ'S ARRIVAL

Alain and Margaret in Port Aransas with JJ

ceilings, so you walked in and saw all these balloons with streamers hanging down. JJ went nuts! He chased around any that came low enough, and he could pick them up in his mouth and shake them around without popping them. I'd never seen anything like it!

From that moment on, if JJ ever needed entertainment, all we had to do was blow up a balloon, and he would be so happy.

The birth of Maggies

2012-19

Life was great while travelling with Alain, but after working for many years, I found myself a bit lost without meaningful challenges. This new retirement life required many adjustments, and I could feel myself ageing rapidly at the age of sixty-nine.

While in Australia in 2012, we often browsed local markets, and I found unique sarongs made from the most beautiful fabrics. I had always loved wearing sarongs and was so surprised that there weren't many ways to wear them without tying big, bulky knots, which were unflattering if one had a few extra pounds of flesh.

After returning to Dallas, this dilemma prompted me to check what

Margaret and Alain, 2012

products were available in the USA. I was shocked to find nothing apart from some wooden buckles, which rarely worked. I was certain that I could find a much better idea, so I started to think of a solution. I still had all my previous wholesale contacts, and I checked with a magnet factory, figuring that this might solve my problem.

Branding for My Maggies

After finding a magnet manufacturer with a 'ball magnet', I was encouraged, as I knew flat magnets would not work because of the lateral solid 'pull'. When I also saw a ring magnet, I thought that might work perfectly. They were expensive, which did not bother me as they were initially intended for personal use on my sarongs in Australia.

My order arrived just a few days later, and I immediately started experimenting. My hunch of putting the ring and ball magnet together had the necessary holding power, so I made a strapless top with a piece of fabric, and it looked great. I went off shopping at the local supermarket where everything stayed in place until I returned to the car and as soon as it opened the car door, the vehicle stole the ring magnet, and my top fell off!

On my next attempt, I tried the ball magnet on the outside. Of course, the shopping cart grabbed the ball magnet, and this time, the ring magnet dropped on the concrete pavement and shattered into a million tiny treacherous shards of glass-like metal. Another no! Flat neodymium magnets are incredibly brittle and easily shatter if dropped.

THE BIRTH OF MAGGIES

I knew I was onto something, and after giving it more thought, I could solve both problems; if the ball magnet was worn on the inside of the fabric and something metal was worn on the outside, it would work. I discovered the perfect answer in a hardware store: a metal washer with an inside diameter about the same size as the magnet circumference. *Yes! Yes! Yes!* I knew that this would be perfect! That revelation occurred on October 20, 2012, and I knew immediately that I had solved a problem women had been facing for a long time. I immediately went to my patent attorney to present the product as 'Patent Pending'. I decided that this was something I could do without employees and, as the product was so small, I could fit all the necessary inventory in a single unused bedroom in my house, so I incorporated it.

This time, I started with a decent investment and was able to self-fund the business. I had enough to cover hiring a professional graphics company from the outset, so I worked with them to develop a great name and logo that would suit the product. I filed for an LLC under the name My Maggies. Alain was a tremendous support and a great sounding board for my ideas. I knew of a significant trade show that as coming up at the Javits Centre in New York, and if I could be ready to have a booth by January 6, 2013, I could launch there.

Maggies brochure, 2013

Within two months, my graphics company had done professional photo shoots with experienced models, a brochure for a handout, and designed packaging so I could make that show. I had such fantastic feedback and knew this product would be a winner.

At the Maggies booth with Keith

I knew I had to immediately launch a website and start working on a video because the product needed a demonstration, and it was extremely tiring to do it all myself.

I had some local women help me with assembly and packaging and was soon getting re-orders.

I attended more trade shows in major markets that year, and I was grateful that I had done so many shows for my previous businesses because I knew the ropes well.

In my first year, I made nearly $50,000 in wholesale sales, with inventory and marketing as my main expenses. In the following years, I continued to find new and creative ways to wear Maggies and innovative ways to sell them.

My focus was on selling to boutiques through trade shows, and my two permanent showrooms were at the World Trade Centre in Dallas and the Atlanta Market Centre. I also increased my list of stores and developed a network of sales representatives as I had decided that this company was to be one hundred per cent wholesale and would not sell to consumers directly.

Alain's illness

2014

I continued working from home with my product line, but Alain's failing health, with significant leg wounds, required much of my nursing experience, so I suspended trade shows and all absences to care for him for most of 2014. As a long-standing sufferer of gout, he had developed osteomyelitis—a bone infection—in his toe. This had begun to spread further and finally caused him to become bedridden. There was concern that he may lose his leg, so I tended to him daily, and when changing his dressings, the flesh had been eaten away to the point where I could see his bone. It was the worst wound case I had seen in my life, and it was so awful that it was happening to the man I loved.

We were living an hour's drive from Dallas, so getting him to and from medical appointments was hard, especially when he became relatively immobile. By the end of 2014, Alain decided he would sign up for hospice in-home care. I was able to access morphine for him and administer it whenever necessary, although he never wanted it.

During this time, I was grateful that Alain had allowed me to redesign his home so that he could live there as long as possible, regardless of mobility challenges. I designed the house so the bedroom was right on the lake, and you could see the sunrise in the morning and the sun glow in the evening. Once he could not move freely about the house, our friends Sara Lee and Don would come and sip cocktails at his bedside to keep him company.

JJ loved being in bed with Alain and was always with him. He would hop down for food or to go outside for a bathroom break, then loyally wander back to the side of the bed, and I would have to lift him back up as he couldn't jump that high on his own. The two of them lay together 24/7.

With Alain's fast decline, I arranged for my sister Jen to visit us in March 2015. It was snowing like crazy the day she arrived, and as I couldn't go into Dallas to pick her up, my accountant collected her for me and brought her down to the lake. Jen arrived, and Alain quickly lost consciousness. He didn't even get to say "hello".

He remained in that condition for a few days, and on March 4, he passed away. I felt like he wanted to wait until someone was there to care for me and until he was comfortable letting go, knowing I was not alone. It was a testament to who he was as a man that he thought of others even on his deathbed. Suddenly, the man who was the life of every party was no longer with me. I provided home care for him until his final moment. The week after his death, we had a fantastic farewell memorial service in the lovely home he had built at Cedar Creek Lake.

Business growth

2014-18

After Alain's death, I moved back to my apartment in Dallas, where I had a double garage. This enabled me to store my inventory and pack and ship orders.

My Maggies LLC had a convenient new headquarters. I started making up for lost time, planning the company's future, and writing to the Home Shopping Network and enrolling in their American Dreams Program. After being introduced to Maggies, they placed a trial order and arranged for my guest appearance at the Florida studio. While on air for a few minutes, the entire order sold out.

HSN onair, 2016

This was the beginning of increasingly larger orders and more on-air appearances. By then, I was ordering more frequently from my Chinese supplier and adding new versions of Maggies to the line.

MY FIRST EVER CAMPING TRIP

Later that year, I came back to Australia for a visit, and while talking to John, he was surprised that I had never been camping before. As a veteran camper, he was quite appalled and made it his mission to correct that oversight. He found Jen and me a pup tent, and Su, John, and I set off for the beautiful Girraween National Park.

It was so lovely and easy. The space and fresh air gave me another product idea—Maggie Snaps! Jen and I were side by side in this pup tent with absolutely no privacy, and as much as I love my sister, I thought, *wouldn't it be nice if there was a way to hang a sheet partition up between us so I don't have to look at her all night long?* My mind started ticking over how I could use my knowledge of magnetics to make this happen. The design idea work was successful, and after returning to the US, I filed for yet another patent. This item was different as it consisted of a 0.5" neodymium ball magnet and two metal 'O' rings. This allowed the magnet, referred to as the 'host', to be secured to the item and fastened on either side with the 'O' rings.

This allowed for fastening jackets and styling scarves and women's clothing in new ways. The versatility is endless! I realised this would be more than capable of replacing the safety pin patented in 1849. The significant improvement of the Maggie Snaps is that it can provide sturdy fastening without penetrating and damaging the fabric.

Invention and New Product
Exposition Show awards, 2016

ICAN 2016 Awards   Margaret at the 2017 ICAN booth

Maggies, in all their forms, continued to be a success. In June 2016, I exhibited at The Invention and New Product Exposition Show (INPEX) in Pittsburgh, Pennsylvania. By that stage, I had applied for three patents to cover the new versions and applications for Maggies and had 192 boutiques throughout the USA and Canada selling them.

A big break came in sales volume when The Grommet Catalogue placed a large order, and this exposure, along with what I got from trade shows and on-air appearances at the Home Shopping Network in Tampa, Florida, ensured speedy growth.

I could keep up with the orders with the help of some friends who packaged the products for me. The time came to begin purchasing inventory packaged to my specifications in China, as that was the only place where neodymium magnets were manufactured. It made sense to start having them ready to ship as well.

With each new product I added to the line, the recognition for my inventions continued to grow. At the ICAN 2016 International Invention Innovation competition in Toronto, Canada, I received many more awards and recognition, sending my sales and demand for the products up every day.

While I was heavily involved with my growing business back home in Australia, my brother John received more accolades. He was made an Officer of the Order of Australia (AO) in 2016 for distinguished service to conservation and the environment through advocacy and leadership roles with various organisations and to natural resource management and protection.

Maggies were, and still are, the only patented magnetic textile fastener that can be used on any fabric, from the finest silks to thick and heavy towelling and furs, without damaging or penetrating the fabric like pins or stitching.

American Dreams Star Award, 2017

Maggies could also close jackets or cardigans, hold scarves and shawls in place, and do many more things like no other product. Twenty-eight thousand packaged units of Maggies were sold in 2016, and I was awarded the coveted 2017 American Dreams Star Award.

I never intended to sell to the consumer market to further assist with the traffic from customers through the products' exposure on TV and word of mouth. However, in 2016, I decided I could direct any traffic from the website if I had an Amazon Seller Account. I set one up, including my product listings, and within a very short time, I had to ship suitable quantities of products to Amazon, where they were delivered to the consumer within two days with free shipping.

Amazon sales allowed me to continue without employees. I employed casual workers who were instrumental in packaging some of the inventory items that were not being packaged at the factory in China. They worked from home, and I paid them per unit packed.

Maggies sold over $1.25 million in wholesale sales between 2013 and 2017, and it was time to start getting things to make my return to Australia possible.

John had been advising me to hasten my return home as his health was failing. That decision was not tricky without children or a partner; my Australian citizenship was still in place. I was pleased I never gave up my Australian citizenship and remained a US permanent resident for my entire absence. I also found it much more practical to change my surname back to Sinclair from Alivizatos as it was easier for others to correct the spelling.

Even so, closing my personal life and business after such a long time away wasn't easy. In 2018, at seventy-six, though I was still running Maggies, I began preparing for my departure. I started by selling and preparing my condominium and personal assets while thinking about my plans to return home again.

MARGARET ANNE

One might consider former nurse, Margaret Sinclair, a serial entrepreneur as she currently holds ten patented inventions, offering solutions to a multitude of problems and needs. With over fifty years of work experience (twenty-three years in nursing and thirty-four years in business), she has not only invented products but has also established her own manufacturing facilities. These facilities have allowed her to deliver her inventions to the world with innovative, intuitive and diverse marketing and business techniques—looking beyond today and far into the future.

A feature story on Maggies from Issue 4 of *Where Women Create Work*

SINCLAIR

Photography by Jesse Scofield

I was born in Australia where I began my nursing career and graduated as a registered nurse, midwife and pediatric nurse. I have since lived more than half my life in Dallas, Texas since being recruited to Baylor University Medical Center in 1971. While working in the Cardiac Surgery unit at I simultaneously trained to become a cardiopulmonary bypass technician for a position with the professor at the University of Athens, Greece from 1973-75. On my return to the United States, I was appointed to Head Nurse in the Neonatal ICU at Massachusetts General Hospital prior to moving to the Medical College of Virginia as a coordinator for the neonatal and pediatric ICUs. My husband's medical training in cardiac surgery was the primary reason for our many international moves between 1974 and 1984.

In 1981, while living in London, I designed a positioning product for premature babies while in a neonatal ICU. I also developed a successful direct patient study at the University College Hospital. I eventually began producing the product from my home and selling it to hospitals across Europe. In 1984, we returned to Dallas where my husband started Baylor's heart transplant program. With no previous business experience, I brazenly started a business to develop and distribute a line of products for patient positioning. In the following fifteen years, I received seven patents from the U.S. Patent and Trademark Office for inventions I had designed for patient positioning.

In 1986, I was named "Woman Business Owner of the Year" by The Association of Women Entrepreneurs of Dallas, and in 1987, I was nominated for the "Ernst and Young Entrepreneur of the Year Award," as well as, receiving an award from Service Corp of Retired Executive for my business ventures. Since then, I continued manufacturing, with up to twenty employees, selling my products to major companies such as Toys 'R Us, Burlington Coat Factory, Costco, Baby Super Stores, and Disney, as well as, major medical catalogues and hospitals. I also established a national network of sales representatives to market and distribute my product lines.

In 1995, while continuing to market to the medical profession, I began designing women's apparel under the name of Masinali Originals and sold my creations to boutiques. The

manufacturing business I created handled designing, cutting and sewing all of the products for both the clothing and medical product industries, which continued over the next ten years. I then sold one of my patents, along with my medical manufacturing business, and opted to retire after having worked for forty-five years—looking forward to more traveling and relaxation.

However, in 2012, while visiting my family in Australia, I recognized there wasn't a convenient and attractive way to wear sarongs—other than to tie bulky, unflattering knots or use some type of pins. So, after returning to Dallas, I began experimenting with magnets to find a solution to this need. In October, I came up with what has become my most exciting invention—a magnetic textile fastener. I immediately applied for my eighth U.S. patent. This invention was so important to me that at the age of sixty-nine I came out of retirement to re-enter the business world once again, but this time taking a huge risk by financing this new business with my retirement savings!

I launched MY MAGGIES, LLC in January 2013 from my home and began selling Maggies (multipurpose magnetic fasteners) at accessory shows and boutiques in New York, Dallas, Atlanta and Las Vegas. Maggies were very well received with an impressive reorder rate, which confirmed my intuition that this product was a "winner". I continued to attend trade shows, though my marketing efforts necessarily were interrupted for nearly a year when I took time out to be a full-time caregiver to my ailing partner.

WISE WORDS

"Creativity is intelligence having fun."

—ALBERT EINSTEIN

In June 2015, I was the recipient of three invention awards at the INPEX Invention Show in Pittsburg where I won a gold medal, the "Midas Touch Award" and the prestigious "Martin Burger Founders Award" with several more awards from the ICAN International Invention Awards in Toronto, Canada in 2016.

The ingenuity of Maggies is the unique combination of a ball magnet to a metal ring, and when separated and reconnected, it securely holds multiple layers of fabric together without damaging even the finest fabric fibers—unlike any other available product. This invention was designed to make it possible to wear a flat piece of fabric such as shawls, scarves and sarongs in a multitude of new ways. Women of all ages and sizes can use Maggies as a wardrobe staple—my ultimate goal is to make MAGGIES a recognized household brand name like "Kleenex" is to tissues.

When I launched Maggies, it was important to me, because of my age, that I not grow the business too quickly so I avoided social media and concentrated on wholesale only to over 250 specialty boutiques and catalogues.

My first major account was The Grommet, which generated great sales with their video product presentations. I found that because of the uniqueness of these products, with absolutely no comparable competition, the product needed constant demonstration to be fully understood. My marketing budget was therefore focused on professionally produced videos, digital materials and trade shows to support this.

BUSINESS GROWTH

Maggies' big break came in June 2016 when I completed an online application to the Home Shopping Network program. The product was put through vigorous testing prior to accepting Maggies into the program. My first trip to the Home Shopping Network studios, "On Air," with master host Bob Circosta was in October 2016. We were quickly rewarded by selling out of our sample order within minutes. In April 2018, I was honored to receive the "HSN Star Award" for the program in recognition for selling 28,000 units of product in 2017. The Home Shopping Network has continued to promote Maggies since then, and my most recent appearance sold over 4,000 units in a 15-minute spot with the assistance of Colleen Lopez.

Having made my decision to concentrate on wholesale only for Maggies, I have been able to grow this company at a strong but steady pace, manageable to me with cash flow financing the growth. This has, in turn, allowed more time for product development. After all, my products are not meant for the short-term but to be useful and available to the world a century from now long after I am gone. After recently having my 75th birthday, I am confident, with so many decades of experience in product development, the path I have chosen for Maggies is the best way to make this product a forever item—making the Maggies brand recognized all over the world just like Velcro and Zippers.

CHOOSE SUCCESS

Pay as much attention to the future as to the present.

Plan, plan and plan and know where you want to be two, five and ten years ahead.

Know your product as well as the market potential.

Don't be afraid to change course when necessary.

Build a strong foundation for the future so that valuable energy is never wasted.

Always plan for cash flow to effectively manage growth without running out of necessary resources.

MAGGIES is protected by the following US PATENTS, which will not expire until 2033.
US Patent #9,320,328
US Patent #9,489,873 B2
US Patent #9,737,102

Trademarks #5573202 for the brand and logo: MAGGIES were issued October 2018

MAGGIE
www.MyMaggies.com

Final return to Australia

2018-23

I spent a full forty-eight years abroad, including just over two years in Greece, three years in London, three years in Boston, three years in Richmond, and the remaining time living and working in Dallas, my first and last home base in the United States.

When I started Maggies, I knew I must make an exit plan one day. Still, I had been focusing on bringing a new product to market and educating the users on this brand-new concept, which needed demonstration and instructions. Maggies had enjoyed significant growth due to my efforts, but I knew there was so much more potential.

It became apparent that I was at a crossroads, requiring a considerable decision: invest more money in inventory, employee training, and moving to a warehouse or move back to Australia and hand over the reins to someone who had the business and marketing skills required to continue the company's rapid growth.

In 2018, I made several trips to Australia to visit the family and make plans to find a home for my return while continuing to search for a successor for Maggies. I underestimated how hard it would be to find people with the necessary skills and ability to take on the company and the market I had created. Achieving the level of success I envisioned for the product would require an individual with exceptional passion and commitment.

The Sinclair siblings, 2017

During one of my visits to my two-level unit on the creek at Currimundi, I realised that because of the stairs, it would be impractical as a 'rest of my life' home. I started looking for alternatives. While back in Dallas, I was searching online when I came across a beautiful over-50s development by Living Choice in Kawana, which also overlooks a creek. I decided to inspect it as soon as possible.

At that time, John had been receiving cancer treatment in Sydney. After talking to him, we decided I could fly back through Sydney and accompany him to Queensland by train, as his doctors had forbidden him to fly back home. Within twenty-four hours, I was on my way. Spending that time with John and enjoying a Christmas dinner with the family was wonderful.

After returning to Dallas, I signed a contract with Living Choice for my new home, a beautiful unit on the water with patios front and back. This enabled me to see the most incredible sunrises and sunsets without setting foot outside. I have lived on the water since 1996; my new home was perfect.

FINAL RETURN TO AUSTRALIA

I signed a contract to list my Currimundi property before returning to the US, and on my return to Dallas, I was notified that I had a buyer. The transition was smooth, as the Currimundi unit sold quickly, and the purchase in Kawana went through without a hitch.

I had packed everything up at Currimundi before I left, and my brother, Chris, arranged to move everything to Kawana.

Unfortunately, John died just a month after my return to Dallas. With everything already underway to make my permanent return home, I was unable to attend his funeral. Instead, I made plans to return in March and arrived the night before his memorial service.

I am so proud of my brother, who passed on March 3, 2019. Through tireless perseverance in his lifelong battle for K'gari, he made Australia a better place. The famous line from John Fitzgerald Kennedy's inaugural speech in 1961 always rang true for me when it came to John: "Ask not what your country can do for you, but what you can do for your country". If that does not reflect the actions of, John, I don't know what would. His extended mission was to do something extraordinary for the country he loved at any cost.

John was a fantastic man, a rebellious son, a loving father, brother, and mentor to me. In certain respects, we were alike as he would address issues or improvements by stepping out of his comfort zone to implement changes. While our parents introduced us to the magic of the island, John's passion for preserving it led to its protection in perpetuity.

∽

My final return was delayed by JJ, whose future was also an important consideration for me. JJ was eleven years old at that stage. I had initially arranged for JJ to stay with friends who had always cared for him while Alain and I were travelling for extended periods, and he was very much at home with the family. However, my friend's circumstances had changed, and as she could not take him, I investigated taking him with me. I was not sure he could stay in quarantine alone for six months.

I found out the Australian quarantine system had been upgraded, and animals could live with their owner as long as they were under the care of an Australian government-approved and certified veterinarian. The vet would also handle the safe transportation of pets from their hometown to Tullamarine Quarantine Station in Victoria.

JJ joined the program on February 14, 2019, and flew out of Dallas on August 14 to meet me in Brisbane. All went seamlessly; my next contact with him was after a 14,000-kilometre trip. When I met him at the Brisbane airport, he looked at me as if to say, "Where on earth have you been? I have been all over the world looking for you."

After I had picked up my wonderful pup and brought him to our new Kawana home, he entered and could not stop rolling over the carpet. He was happy to be home, as was I. It was far less traumatic than I had expected, and JJ was my constant companion until he died soon after he was diagnosed with bladder cancer in August 2023, four years after he arrived in Australia.

As I had not yet found a successor for Maggies in the USA, I managed the business from my new domicile. I forwarded my US mail to a Dallas address, which I could access via email. I forwarded my business phone to Skype In, making me accessible to customers and able to take orders. I would then send the order to the fulfilment centre to ship them to the retailers. I also shipped bulk orders through the Amazon Fulfillment Centre.

Although I was able to manage for sixteen months, this gave me the necessary time to make permanent arrangements in the USA. In 2021, I reluctantly signed a five-year contract to free me from the business. However, I knew it was suboptimal; I was desperate to start living without the company's demands and enjoy being home forever. It was the worst decision I had ever made in my thirty-eight years in business.

I hoped the new owner could pick up and keep the business growing. However, I overestimated their marketability but effectively demonstrated the various ways Maggies could be used. Consequently, their sales have declined through poor marketing and lack of investment, even though I had left them with over US$100,000 worth of saleable inventory. Had I been able to stay just one more year in the USA, Maggies would have continued its upward trend, and I would have introduced several great new additions to the line, which I had been developing.

Returning to Australia was worth the enormous move, so I have no regrets. Being with family again was the best thing I could have done and something I had missed for the forty-eight years I had been absent. Nothing can ever replace one's family.

I still have hope for Maggies. They are one of the only products in the world, that are indestructible, multi-functional, and can be passed on to future generations. In the time they have been available, there has never been a complaint—only compliments on their versatility and usefulness. I still have faith that they will be an excellent product for many decades throughout the world.

Since returning to Australia, my only trip has been a three-week holiday to Greece.

I arrived in May 2022 to observe changes and meet with friends I had not seen since my previous visit in 1978. Of course, the lifestyle in the modern city had changed, but nothing in the ancient town had. Seeing part of it from a tourist perspective was an incredible opportunity.

Catching up with Peter in Greece

I met Peter, who took me to his apartment, a fantastic museum with memoirs of his transplant patients dominating shelves. He was a master of memories and kept mementos of his incredible achievements and every patient. He also remembered the only dog he had ever owned, and there was Sherlock's replica, forever immortalised, lying comfortably on his dog bed next to the precious antique desk his Uncle Gerasimos had left to him.

Peter's tribue to Sherlock

Peter proudly showed me his Australian Army hat, which Chris had gifted to him when we visited Canberra in 1989. Despite its worldly travels, it was in perfect condition and nestled in a drawer. No matter how far and wide he travelled, Peter kept things that would help him remember the most precious times of his life. In contrast, I always endeavoured to travel with minimal possessions—a decision I occasionally regret.

Though thirty years have passed since Peter and I decided to go our separate ways, he has always been readily available when I need his advice and reminders of past events. He will forever be my best friend until death do us part, which, ironically, were the vows we made when we married a half-century ago. It seems that I will always be a Leo, always faithful.

I will always be eternally grateful and blessed that I have been destined to meet and be close to three incredible men who have contributed to and supported me since my overseas journey and had so many years with them as my mentors while supporting and encouraging me on my life's journey. These three brilliant men were great thinkers and have all made outstanding contributions to society:

Peter Alexander. Alivizatos, MD.
Alain Justin Marengo-Rowe, MD.
My brother, Dr. John Sinclair, AO.

I considered every experience of my life a learning opportunity and have never regretted following my instincts.

Having visited Australia regularly since 2005, sometimes for three months at a time, I envisioned my permanent move back to the Sunshine Coast would be a piece of cake. John had always kept me in touch with the family by arranging reunions every visit, so I connected with everyone. But it was quite a surprise for me to discover that, as the only member of the family without children or a partner since Alain's death, I lacked my own 'pod' (descendants). This is often the 'glue' in one's later years.

Fortunately, I still have many great friends abroad, and thanks to Skype, WhatsApp, and social media, I can communicate freely with them wherever and whenever I choose. Since returning, I have also met some wonderful friends and neighbours and built a new friendship group on the Coast.

Not many people in their eighties are still familiar with today's technology. Still, as I grew my various businesses over the decades, I have been at the forefront of adapting to everything from computers and software to emails, cell phones, social media, and credit cards. As soon as something new appeared, I learned how to master it to grow my business.

Ultimately, this allowed me to write and publish my story at the age of eighty-one without too much difficulty.

My new life has given me time to study more practical advancements, focusing on living a healthy, pain-free life without prescription medications. I am learning so much about the science of aging while using food as medicine. I am looking forward to my final twenty-five-plus years in optimal health, with my new goal of becoming an octogenarian like my Aunty Flo, who lived to 101.

My connection to K'gari through Kingfisher Bay

2025

I am eighty-one as I write this book. While in my youth with my parents living in Talinga, it was easy to come and go, but as the years passed and without ready access to a 4WD vehicle, I still have the desire to reconnect with the island that I still call home, I have discovered that I could be there as often as I felt the need to reconnect with Mum, Dad and John whose spirits remain on K'gari. I have found staying at the fabulous Kingfisher Bay Resort on the island's western side much more effortless.

I can go anytime alone or with friends at any time I choose, not depending on the tides or others. I can drive myself to the River Heads at Hervey Bay, which takes less than three hours from my home on the Sunshine Coast. After checking my bag at the mainland office, I take the ferry/barge across to Kingfisher to find my luggage waiting for me when I go to my pre-checked accommodation. The beauty of staying there makes it so relaxing and effortless, with all the comforts of home without having to self-cater, with three superb restaurants, three bars, three swimming pools and spa plus much more, that cater to all ages.

The resort features the K'gari World Heritage Discovery Centre, which the University of the Sunshine Coast created in partnership with Kingfisher

The K'gari World Heritage Discovery Center at the Kingfisher Bay Resort

A dedicated plaque to John within the Discovery Centre

Bay Resort. They dedicated the Centre to John and his work. I always feel proud when I visit, see this acknowledgment of my brother's work and spend moments of reflection and solitude with him.

In addition to excellent, comfortable accommodations, Kingfisher Resort offers several tourist bus tours with knowledgeable guides for safe, comfortable visits to the island's beauty spots, including Eurong where visitors can see Talinga perched on the sand hill.

Another benefit is the seasonal whale watching trips and the store, art gallery, and spa services.

For more information on Kingfisher Resort, visit www.kingfisherbay.com.

Epilogue: A legacy of connection

2024-25

My nephew Andres' wedding was nothing short of magical. Held at Eurong Beach, it was a rare celebration where family, history, and the island's spirit intertwined seamlessly. As I sat at the poolside reception, the ocean serenading us and the full moon casting its silver glow, I couldn't help but feel an overwhelming sense of connection to this place and its role in our family's story.

In February 2024, Andres, the adopted son of my late brother John, stood with his new bride, Jingwen, under the clear night sky, surrounded by loved ones. It struck me then: none of us would be here if it weren't for the house my father built—Talinga. That house wasn't just a building perched high on a hill overlooking the sea; it was the foundation of a legacy that connected us all to this island. I looked up at Talinga, illuminated by the moonlight, and realised it was my family's story.

Sharan, his adopted mother, suddenly and tragically passed the prior year, making Andres' wedding even more poignant. As I watched him celebrate this new chapter, I felt a more profound closeness to him—a bond strengthened by our shared love for John and this island.

TALINGA

Andres and Jingwen's beach wedding

My thoughts wandered back to Talinga's origins. My father purchased one of the first pieces of land issued for building on K'gari and chose a spot that touched the heavens. Talinga means sandhill, a fitting name for a house built from the island's materials. With the help of family and friends, Dad crafted each brick by hand, mixing island sand and water with concrete brought from the mainland. Like the house, those bricks became symbols of resilience and determination—qualities my father passed down to all of us.

I remember helping Dad with the bricks during my visits from Brisbane, Sydney, Perth and Athens. Those moments involved laughter, physical exertion, and a common goal. The house was constructed brick by brick, like how our family's connection with the island developed. Over the years, Talinga became more than a house; it became a gathering place, a refuge, and a symbol of our shared history.

As the oldest surviving member of Mum and Dad's five children, I feel a profound responsibility to preserve our family's story. Each generation has found joy, peace, and inspiration at Talinga. For us, it is not just a house—it symbolises our collective values and memories. Seeing Andres and his bride start their new journey reminded me that Talinga's legacy is about the past and the future.

EPILOGUE: A LEGACY OF CONNECTION

When I returned home after the wedding, I looked at a painting my mother had brought me as a gift years ago. It depicts Talinga standing proud against the backdrop of K'gari's natural beauty. Like the house it represents, that painting tells a story of love, perseverance, and connection—a story I was determined to share in this book and feature on this cover.

Reflecting on that night at Eurong Beach, I realise the full circle of our family's journey. From Dad's dream of building a house on the island to John's unwavering commitment to its preservation, K'gari has been a constant in our lives. Even though at the time of writing Jennifer, Chris and I are the only surviving children of Beryl and Charlie, we have seen the evolution of Talinga from the original patch of the earth in 1964 to the present in 2025. We know our parents' vision for Talinga and neighbouring Weerona will endure because of the shareholders who contribute to the ongoing maintenance of the properties. Their support ensures future generations of people who visit from around the world will benefit from soaking up the majesty of our little patch of paradise.

When anyone stays at Talinga, they will see a table in the corner of the main room—a seemingly ordinary piece of furniture, yet its history is anything but. My parents, Beryl and Charles Sinclair acquired this table when they married. It became a fixture of our lives, moving with us from house to house and settling in its rightful place at Talinga, the home Dad built with his hands.

This table has witnessed decades of family meals, spirited card games, and quiet conversations. It has seated every single person who has visited Talinga, from friends and family to international guests and even a few

The dining table being protected for posterity

famous faces. In a way, this table is the beating heart of our family's story—sturdy, enduring, and filled with memories.

It's impossible to think about the table without recalling the day Cyclone Daisy struck in 1972. Talinga, perched at the island's highest point and fully exposed to the elements, took the brunt of the storm. Dad, ever resourceful, piled the furniture—including the table—against a wall to brace the structure. His quick thinking saved the roof from blowing off, a catastrophe that would have devastated the house. The effort nearly cost him his life. The cyclone's ferocity left him unable to walk correctly or use his hands for months. Yet he persevered, embodying the resilience that defines our family and Talinga itself.

Over the years, the table has transformed into a work of art. Layers of paint stripped back during restoration revealed a colourful, abstract history beneath the surface. It's now coated in a transparent protective layer, preserving its character while making it a practical centrepiece for daily use. Each mark and groove tells a story: countless games, laughter of children, adult debates, and meals shared by travellers. Famous actresses, conservationists and members of various committees have all sat at this table, their conversations blending into the rich tapestry of Talinga's history.

Today, Talinga and Weerona are managed by fifty shareholders, ensuring they continue to thrive. The addition of a deck in recent years has only enhanced its charm, offering the perfect spot to watch the sunrise over the ocean—a daily masterpiece that reminds us of the island's magic.

To book a holiday at Talinga or Weerona and experience the island paradise for yourself, visit **www.kgariholidaylodges.com.au**

Talinga today

About the author

Margaret Sinclair began her career in Australia as a registered nurse, midwife, and paediatric nurse before moving to the USA in 1971. There, she continued her career in Dallas, Athens, Boston, and Richmond before moving to London in 1981 and returning to Dallas again in 1984. While working in a neonatal unit in London, she designed her first invention—a positioning product for premature babies.

After returning to Dallas in 1984, she started a manufacturing business to develop and distribute her line of patient positioning products. The U.S. Patent and Trademark Office awarded her seven patents for patient and infant positioning inventions.

Margaret Sinclair

In 1986, she received the Woman Business Owner of the Year award from The Association of Women Entrepreneurs of Dallas. In 1987, she was a nominee for the Ernst and Young Entrepreneur of the Year award, and she also received an award from S.C.O.R.E. for her business ventures.

Margaret continued to grow her manufacturing business and sold it to major retailers. Simultaneously, she designed, patented, and developed a line of patient positioning products sold through medical distributors, hospitals, and medical catalogues. She also established national networks of sales representatives to market and distribute her product line in the healthcare and retail industries.

In 1995, she began designing women's apparel, which she manufactured along with medical and retail outlets and marketed her line of Masinali Originals. In 2005, she sold one of her patents and medical manufacturing business and retired from business.

In October 2012, while vacationing at the beach, she saw a need for a way to fasten sarongs, and after discovering that there was no way other than tying a knot, using a pin or stitching the fabric, she set out to find a way to accomplish this task. When Margaret came across the ball magnet, she quickly associated it with a ring, found the answer to the problem, and filed for her eighth patent, issued in 2016, to be followed by a ninth and tenth soon after.

She decided to test this product in the market to see how it would sell, so she founded My Maggies, LLC. On January 6, 2013, she launched her product to retailers at the Accessory Show at the Jacob Javits Convention Center in New York.

Since starting Maggies, she has been awarded numerous Patent Awards at the Inpex Show in Pittsburgh and the ICAN Invention Show in Toronto.

She chose to be a wholesale manufacturer and sold her products to nearly 300 retailers in the USA, Canada, and Australia, as well as through her store on Amazon USA. Her major break in marketing Maggies was when she made several appearances on the Home Shopping Network in Tampa, FL. She also won the HSN Star Award for exceptional vendor achievement. Hopefully, Maggies will one day become as common as Velcro and zippers and become a go-to product for innovative ways in which clothing is worn. Unfortunately, her marketing efforts in the USA were cut short when, at 75, she returned to Australia.

www.masinali.com

References

1. Shipping in the big blow: Maheno mystery' *The Cairns Post*. Cairns, Queensland. 10 July 1935. p. 7. Archived from the original on 11 August 2022. Retrieved 21 November 2012 – via National Library of Australia.

2. Thorpe, Vanessa (3 October 2021). "Two princesses, a royal dressmaker and a row about a wedding gown". *The Guardian*. Archived from the original on 3 October 2021. Retrieved 3 October 2021.

3. Cansdale, Dominic, 'Paula Stafford, the iconic Gold Coast designer who brought the bikini to Australia, dies aged 102.' June 22, 2022, retrieved on February 3, 2025 from https://www.abc.net.au/news/2022-06-23/gold-coast-businesswoman-bikini-designer-paula-stafford-dies/101174424

4. 'Seven die in bus crash on island.' *The Canberra Times*, July 23, 1970. Retrieved on February 3, 2025 from https://trove.nla.gov.au/newspaper/article/110333422

5. Sinclair, John, 'Fighting for Fraser Island.' Kerr Publishing, 1994.

6. Brown, Kenneth (1974). "Greece". *The World Book Year Book 1974*. Chicago: Field Enterprises Educational Corporation.

7. Fiddler, Alesia, 'When the Olympian King married his Danish bride: How sailing gold medallist Constantine of Greece tied the knot with Queen Anne-Marie 60 years ago in gilded Athens ceremony... and Princess Anne was a bridesmaid.' Daily Mail UK, September 18, 2024. Retrieved on January 1, 2025 from https://www.dailymail.co.uk/news/royals/article-13751035/King-Constantine-Greece-Anne-Marie-wedding.html

8. Turkish invasion of Cyprus, New World Encyclopedia. Retrieved on January 1, 2025 from https://www.newworldencyclopedia.org/entry/Turkish_invasion_of_Cyprus

9. 'Fraser Island Brumbies,' Fraser Tours. Retrieved on January 1, 2025 from https://fraser-tours.com/article/Brumbies-on-fraser-island

10. 'Australian Dingo,' Dingo Den. Retrieved on January 1, 2025 from https://www.dingoden.net/facts.html

11. 'The Mass General Difference,' Massachusetts General Hospital, retrieved on January 3, 2025 from https://www.massgeneral.org/about

12. *Operation Sail 1976*. Official Program Book by Intercom Interrelated Communications Corp. 1976.

13. Behrendt, Larissa, 'Finding Eliza: Power and colonial storytelling.' University of Queensland Press, 2016.

14. 'Eliza Fraser.' IMDB listing. Retrieved on February 3, 2025 from https://www.imdb.com/title/tt0074466/

15. Welch, Sydney 'Blizzard of '78: 46 years later, a look back at the storm that crippled New England.' 10Boston. Published February 7, 2024. Retrieved on January 3, 2025 from https://www.nbcboston.com/weather/stories-weather/blizzard-of-78-46-years-later-a-look-back-at-the-storm-that-crippled-new-england/3272221/

16. Jones, Charles, 'The Organ Thieves: The Shocking Story of the First Heart Transplant in the Segregated South. Simon and Schuster, 2020.

17. Nathoo, Ayesha, 'The operation that took medicine into the media age.' BBC, Centre for Medical History, University of Exeter, December 3, 2017.

18. "Argentine to reaffirm Sovereignty Rights over The Falkland Islands". *National Turk*. January 4, 2012. Archived from the original on July 7, 2019.

19. On This Day 1950-2005. BBC Home, '1982: IRA bombs cause carnage in London.' Retrieved on January 3, 2025 from http://news.bbc.co.uk/onthisday/hi/dates/stories/july/20/newsid_2515000/2515343.stm

20. Hummel III, Joe, 'The introduction of the World Wide Web: Birth of the modern internet.' Pop Culture Madness, published April 30, 1993. Retrieved on January 8, 2025 from https://popculturemadness.com/the-introduction-of-the-world-wide-web-birth-of-the-modern-internet.

21. 'Celebrating thirty years of world heritage,' FINIA retrieved on January 9, 2015 from https://finia.org.au/2022/11/05/celebrating-thirty-years-of-world-heritage/

www.ingramcontent.com/pod-product-compliance
Lightning Source LLC
Chambersburg PA
CBHW061726070526
44583CB00024B/3016